Ahimsa

In the Hindu, Buddhist and Jain tradition,
respect for all living things and avoidance of
violence towards others

Caroline Earle x

Caroline Earle

Grosvenor House
Publishing Limited

The right of Caroline Earle to be identified as the author of this
work has been asserted in accordance with Section 78
of the Copyright, Designs and Patents Act 1988

The book cover is copyright to Caroline Earle

This book is published by
Grosvenor House Publishing Ltd
Link House
140 The Broadway, Tolworth, Surrey, KT6 7HT.
www.grosvenorhousepublishing.co.uk

A CIP record for this book
is available from the British Library

ISBN 978-1-78623-623-4

For Aurora, my little herbivore.
Aurora was the mythical Roman goddess of the dawn.
Let us hope we are at the dawn of a new,
more compassionate world. You might be small,
but you will come to see how big your actions can be and
what difference you can make in your lifetime.

Contents

Foreword

Who knows where any journey undertaken with an open mind and an open heart is going to take you?

When grandmother Caroline Earle embarked on a gap year to mark her semi-retirement in 2018, she fully expected that the months of travel would leave her with a rich store of memories but she cannot have known how profoundly the experience was to change her whole personal outlook, her principles and her way of life.

This inspiring memoir is built around a central story of one woman's conversion to veganism. Not so long ago, that word would have demanded an asterisk and an appended definition explaining the nature of a mysterious eccentricity indulged in by a tiny minority. Today, veganism is rapidly becoming a mainstream choice... but this is not a fashionable lifestyle guide, let alone another cookery book. Instead, it is an uplifting, thought-provoking account of the gentle philosophy that lies behind the trend and the way in which it revealed itself to a hard-headed and sophisticated professional, not least through the simple act of cuddling a cow in India.

In eastern religions, the concept of Ahimsa from which this book takes its title encompasses compassion, non-violence and a desire to do no harm to other living creatures. At a personal level, as in this case, it can signify a commitment to kinder, more mindful living in all respects and, when it comes to food, to the adoption of a plant-based regime including no animal products of any kind.

As dramatic as it has been, Caroline's life-changing epiphany did not quite come out of the clear blue sky of Udaipur. It was, rather, the challenging culmination of a complex web of influences, experiences and wisdom gained over many years as a senior journalist in print and broadcasting and a mother with a sometimes troubled family to nurture and protect. Ahimsa came at the right time and in the right place to make sense of it all.

Readers will meet her family, including Zippy, a rescue dog with his own message to convey about the meaning of life, and David, the retired paramedic husband whose pugnacious sense of justice helped point towards a new spiritual direction as they travelled together through South-East Asia, Sri Lanka and India.

The story of their midlife journey is by turns entertaining, moving, sad and ultimately happy, but this is no airy New Age account of yet another western traveller going east to find herself. Anyone who has known Caroline in her various roles as a journalist and charity fundraiser in her native Jersey is likely to testify to her no-nonsense approach to practical matters, her sometimes slightly scary efficiency and her formidable strength of character.

For that reason, the knowledge that close encounters at an animal sanctuary in a strange land could have such an enduring impact on her life makes this book's vegan message all the more powerful, while those still searching for a personal philosophy of any kind that feels right and recalibrates their world can celebrate the news that there is no age limit on adventure or the chance of a life-changing experience.

Caroline still lives and works in the Channel Islands, a much-blessed and beautiful archipelago just off the coast of France. One of its most renowned residents, Victor Hugo, once observed that there is nothing more powerful than an idea whose time has come.

As the 21st century unfolds, many more will find themselves discovering that veganism is just such an idea.

Chris Bright
Former Editor, Jersey Evening Post

Once upon a time, there was a wise man who used to go to the ocean to do his writing. He had a habit of walking on the beach before he began his work.

One day, as he was walking along the shore, he looked down the beach and saw a human figure moving like a dancer. He smiled to himself at the thought of someone who would dance to the day, and so he walked faster to catch up.

As he got closer, he noticed that the figure was that of a young man, and that what he was doing was not dancing at all. The young man was reaching down to the shore, picking up small objects, and throwing them into the ocean.

He came closer still and called out: 'Good morning. May I ask what it is that you are doing?'

The young man paused, looked up, and replied: 'Throwing starfish into the ocean.'

'I must ask, then, why are you throwing starfish into the ocean?' asked the somewhat startled wise man.

To this, the young man replied: 'The sun is up and the tide is going out. If I don't throw them in, they'll die.'

Upon hearing this, the wise man commented: 'But, young man, do you not realise that there are miles and miles of beach and there are starfish all along every mile? You can't possibly make a difference.'

At this, the young man bent down, picked up yet another starfish, and threw it into the ocean. As it met the water, he said: 'It made a difference for that one.'

— Loren Eiseley,
philosopher and
anthropologist (1907-77)

Medication for the soul

'Animals are my friends and I don't eat my friends'
—George Bernard Shaw

It was the story of the staggering street dog with maggots in his head that has brought us to Udaipur.

A few weeks back we saw a two-minute video on Facebook showing how the rescue team at Animal Aid Unlimited saved a dog's life in the nick of time. We didn't hesitate to add the animal sanctuary to our flexible schedule.

Primarily we are here for the dogs, but we are surprised by how much we are touched, literally and spiritually, by all of the other animals.

One of the first things that most volunteers experience is bottle-feeding the calves. My first one is pure white, with the softest hair you can imagine. She nudges in to me, gulps down her milk and comes back for more. Afterwards, she stays for a cuddle, her milky breath in my face.

On any typical day one of our tasks — indicated by the hand-drawn red heart on the whiteboard — is to 'give love' to the sheep and brush them. Some allow this, but there are *two young brown ones who are not so sure. To be honest, sheep have never done much for me, probably because I have never got to know one. Usually they are skittish and run away, and their coat is hard and wiry so they are not actually that nice to touch.*

But here is my first lesson. While I am sitting amongst the calves one morning, a sheep comes over to say hello. (We are always saying hello to the animals.) It is always nice when an animal comes to you for attention, rather than the other way around.

I duly say hello. She looks me in the eyes. There is a moment when you seem to communicate with an animal, when you acknowledge something special, and you just stay with it for as long as you can. You know it isn't really personal, but you like to think it is.

When you look into a pair of huge brown eyes, you can't help but wonder what goes on in the animal's mind. It reminds us that animals are sentient beings, capable of feeling. It seems obvious but, as with many simple truths, we sometimes need reminding.

The sheep stays there for a chat and a rubdown. And I love it. I am surprised by how gentle a creature she is.

I never cease to be amazed by how many animals are open to trusting a human being again, despite what has happened to them... the donkey who has been beaten about the face (a court case is pending), the cow who has had acid thrown on her, the dog who has been tied up with wire around her jaw for so long that she is permanently scarred.

And then you get another lesson when you find the courage to sit next to a huge water buffalo or brush the flank of a super-sized bull. In the cow and donkey sanctuary in the early afternoon heat, we get to brush the animals. I don't think most of them really need brushing, but it is a good way to bring us closer to them — and they seem to like it.

When a young, but still impressively large, water buffalo comes to you, it is very special indeed. Their skin is tough and the hair on the back of their wrinkly necks is long but thin. They like being brushed, much like I imagine they like having a bird on their back to pick off the bugs.

The one I am drawn to has a small tuft of white hair on her head and she is called Flower.

There is a large bull who is interested in being brushed. At first, when he walks over, I shy away, especially as he tends to shift others out of his way with his horns. Soon I realise that he is just jealous, so I pluck up the courage to brush him and he stays there contentedly until he has had enough and ambles off.

The sanctuary area for cows and donkeys is a peaceful place, with plenty of room for the animals to relax. When they are standing still or lying down, you don't see their disability. It is only when they move that you notice the amount of limping and hobbling, or where limbs are missing. Most donkeys have one if not both front ankles bandaged from where they have been tied up for too long. They are, however, very capable of leaning on those two front feet if they need to give a swift kick from the back, to any animal that mildly irritates them.

There is another enclosure where cattle and donkeys are recovering, which includes the 'accident and emergency' area. One cow has a lot of bandaging around her head. We see the staff changing the dressing. As a veteran paramedic, David's instinct is to get a closer look. Over 25 years he has seen things which are best described as surreal. The large hole where the eye socket should be is astonishing but the animal doesn't seem to be in any pain while the staff *irrigate it with saline. We understand that maggots have already eaten the nerve endings.*

This, David says, really is surreal.

In this part of the sanctuary we can sit with a dying cow. In India, cows are sacred and it is against the law for one to be put down. All that staff can do is ease their suffering with medication. One black cow is brought in with a broken back from which she can never recover. She is lying in the shade on a black plastic mat, where she is kept as comfortable as possible. It is only a matter of time.

And, if volunteers have the time, they can sit with her. David sits with her for quite a while, stroking her strangely cold head, talking gently, reassuring her and batting flies away. It is a humbling and moving experience. It seems deliberate on the part of a large black and white horned bull that he sits himself right next to her. At one point he licks her face. We don't think they have been brought in together, but I hope she feels comforted by his presence. She is not there the next morning.

It's in the hours before death that you can only hope that the magnificent creature in front of you knows that it is not alone. It is cared about, it is loved. This perhaps is the purest definition of the word 'namaste'. I see the beauty of your soul.

Cow 17 is my favourite. She is young. I have no idea about her history, but she is ridiculously friendly. To while away half an hour with her, lying in the straw, with her head nuzzled in to your chest, is heaven on earth. Her face next to mine, she smells like she has eaten candy floss. Her big brown eyes, just gorgeous.

I promise her I will never eat animals again.

I even learn some cow physio. Volunteers like me require no animal or medical background to do this, just a shed-load of common sense, love and compassion. And time. Time seems to stand still when your entire focus is a cow which is recovering from injury, usually the result of a traffic accident. The daily routine involves checking the whiteboard for which animals need attention, and making sure you are rubbing their muscles to get the blood circulating, or just giving them a lovely massage around their shoulders.

Towards the end of our stay, I do some physio on Cow 109. We are already acquainted as I have massaged her a few times before. She has a broken back leg and some bandaging under her front. She is sitting in the shed and I rub her back and her shoulder, thinking of nothing much. But when I stand up to move to the next animal on the list, the vets come over to lie her down on the floor and swiftly administer a drug. I am not sure what is going on. She seemed fine. My physio shift is ending and I have to go to dog-sit in a different area. I deal with a couple of bouncy dogs, one of whom treads in his poo and transfers it to my neck. (Many a time we share a tuk-tuk back to our homestay and, apologising to the driver, laugh that we are wearing our favourite perfume, Kennel No 5.)

When I return to the cow area that same afternoon, the big black cow has died. I pat all the cows who are down, the grey one is cold, the brown one definitely won't last the night. But oh my God, no, please not 109 — she is too young to die. She was ok. I keep willing her to get up. I ask a vet what has happened. He says she isn't getting up on her feet. I know this is bad news. Barely holding back tears, I go to the calves' enclosure to calm myself down. My favourite calf ambles over as if to reassure me.

Before I finish for the day, I check on the cows once more. 109 has died. I get in the tuk-tuk, put my sunglasses on and cry my heart out all the way home.

Despite having emotional moments with cows, sheep, goats, water buffalo and even a donkey, my favourite times are with the dogs. You can quickly establish a rapport with a dog and I find myself returning to the same disabled dogs in Handicapped Heaven. There are dogs who have lost limbs, most of them have lost the use of their back legs and they are either dragging them behind them or the limbs have been amputated. There is one, Deepak, who has only one and a half legs. He gets about all right. He is a handsome dog, with quite thick rusty brown fur.

Then there are the 'ugly dogs'. It's what they are called for identification purposes but everyone knows that they have even more beautiful souls. They are really friendly, but you can see why they have been rejected. They might have a long tooth protruding forwards, or a misfitting jaw, or no lower jaw at all, leaving the tongue to flop out and get covered in sand when they are lying down.

In a corner I sit with one dog who responds immediately to being touched. Her haunch starts moving like she is scratching her ear, though there is no leg there. I scratch her ear for her. The haunch keeps moving.

Another dog, with longer fur, just rolls over in the sand, inviting a tummy rub. He is so chilled that I find myself playing with him like I would a normal dog, a bit more forcefully and a bit more fun, and it is only later that I realise his back legs are not functioning.

We have been shown how to give the dogs a lovely sooth-ing back massage and how to rub their shoulders — it's where most of them will carry their tension from having to lift their bodies and compensate for their disabilities.

One pretty black dog is called Michael Jackson. He has the most lovely nature but thanks to a neurological deficit his legs are very wobbly. He moves like he is a stringed puppet who has just consumed seven pints of beer. He often falls over as his brain misjudges the distance between his paws and the ground. And when he tries to run, it is cartoon-like in the way his back legs try to get him moving. He never seems to need reassurance but I often give it.

Later in the week we are introduced to the area where it is not known for sure what, if any, diseases the dogs are carrying. We have had our rabies injections so we are allowed in, but we are advised to exercise more caution. Somehow the reward here is even greater. Sitting for ten minutes with a dog who is in a small kennel for his own protection while he heals feels like valuable work. You can make a real difference to their day. Some are so mangy they have not a scrap of fur. One bitch has skin so hard, dry and cracked that she looks like she is half-armadillo. Some wag their tail and you know you can relax with them. Others don't have a tail that can wag any more.

Some dogs press themselves against the back wall of the kennel, keeping as far away as possible, eyeing us suspiciously as we talk to them and tell them how handsome and brave they are. Gradually their natural curiosity overrides their fear and they edge closer until they sniff an outstretched hand. Patience is richly rewarded when a scruffy mutt allows us to stroke his neck or tickle behind his ear.

Some have 'lampshades' on their heads, the plastic cone to stop them from licking a wound. One white dog is so nervous of me that I cannot touch him. But he is ok with me just sitting, chatting. It seems perfectly natural to be telling him about my rescue dog back home. I change his matting, top up his water and leave him just a bit better than he was ten minutes before.

An important part of Animal Aid's work is education, teaching people about animal welfare, taking their message into schools and inspiring local communities to protect the lives of all animals. The staff, who also run a programme of spaying, neutering and anti-rabies inoculation, respond to calls to help more than 50 animals every single day.

One of the first things they taught me was in their volunteer manual, where the founders explain how the animals have opened their eyes to what happens in any business that uses animals as commodities — like dairies and poultry farms, the leather industry, and slaughterhouses and laboratories where animals are used in experimentation.

'We love knowing that every volunteer will have a chance to become closer to all animals, and maybe come to new realisations about the privilege of protecting them, including no longer eating them or using them for their products,' the manual reads.

Each day we go back to our homestay sweaty, dirty, sandy, smelling of dogs, with pee and sometimes poo on our clothes, mixed in with dried milk splatters from the calf-feeding, a big smile on our faces and our hearts bursting with love. We are in a place of healing, though we suspect that humans are getting as much healing as the animals, if not more. Over our lunchtime thali, one volunteer describes it as medication for the soul.

Personally, I have never been more 'in the moment' than right here in Udaipur.

Well, if the kids won't leave home...

*'The more that you read,
The more things you will know.
The more that you learn,
The more places you'll go!'*

— *Dr Seuss*

'I can never have enough of India. I long to return.' These are the words of the same woman who welled up at her first sight of the Taj Mahal, saying: 'There are no words... for *that*.' Actress Miriam Margolyes was one of the stars of the TV series The Real Marigold Hotel, where ageing celebrities are sent off to India to see how they might cope with retirement there.

We fell in love with the idea of spending at least three months in the country, but it wasn't until the second series that we hatched a plan. Jealousy grew as we watched the likes of Lionel Blair and Dennis Taylor living for weeks in Kerala. An idea began, a plan started growing, a dream really was going to become reality. We could talk of nothing else.

Already big fans of the original film, The Best Exotic Marigold Hotel, we longed to go to Udaipur, where some of the movie had been filmed. It really did feel like a 'now or never' chance while adult children were settled, grandparenting duties were not yet onerous, and we had saved enough money to quit our jobs.

It wasn't long before we realised that perhaps it was not the best time to visit as we were highly likely to clash with monsoon season. Wet season itself would be ok but, at our age, we felt we should err on the side of caution, especially after watching news coverage of India's worst monsoon in years later in the year. It killed more than 1,000 people and brought down buildings in major cities.

We both admit that there is a part of both me as a journalist and David as a keen amateur photographer (more than the paramedic instincts) which wanted to be there at the time, ready to document as well as help in time of need. Not for the last time were we thinking: 'Maybe if we were 30 years younger.'

Seeing as we were already counting down to the last day at work, we felt we couldn't just shift our plan further into the future and instead we decided to add to the front of the itinerary by visiting other countries before we reached India. Three months became six. We would fly to Bangkok on 1 July 2018 and return just in time for Christmas.

The planning was part of the fun. A full year before departure day, a large map of India found a permanent place in our summer room. That's the posh term for our extension. What we liked to think of as our cosy winter lounge had been taken over as a bedroom for a son who had returned home. One elderly friend regularly lets us know that he thinks we live in a bus station, such are the comings and goings of people in our house.

We added sticky dots to the map to indicate where we wanted to visit, usually in response to something we saw on TV, and we set up our blog, kidswontleavehome.blog.

As part of the preparation for six months in developing countries, David had to research the availability of treatment facilities for his blood-clotting deficiency. At home we take so much for granted, including the fact that Factor 8 treatment for haemophiliacs is readily available. When getting his routine inoculations, he joked with his GP about the availability of such life-saving treatment in places like Vietnam and Cambodia. He asked further about what might happen if he had a significant bleed from being in a car accident, for example, and they laughed that in that sort of scenario essentially it would be game over.

It only served to reinforce his philosophy: You only live once? No, you live each and every day. You die only once, usually not before your allotted time. 'I would rather die with my beloved, doing what I love, than stay at home,' he said. (He assures me that he means me and not his Canon 70D.)

Much as we get on well with each other, we decided that we needed to come up with a safe word in case we were winding each other up while we were on the road. We anticipated that there might be times when we were getting on each other's nerves and we needed a code which we could use to indicate that we just wanted our own time, David might want extra time processing his photos, or I might want to wander off to the nearest market by myself. Actually, the safe word was two words. 'Fuck' and 'off'.

Visas, vaccinations and kit lists had to be ticked off, but what I hadn't had to do when I had travelled to Kathmandu as a teenager more than 30 years ago was make sure the household bills were paid, notify authorities that we would be away, teach the kids where the fuse box was, and make sure Zippy had extra dog-sitters and walkers on his rota.

But we didn't want to over-plan. When we arrived in Bangkok, only one hotel, one train and a one-week stay at the Elephant Nature Park in Chiang Mai were booked. The whole point was to get us out of our comfort zone and David reminded me that the actual travelling between places was very much part of the journey.

Indeed it was. The overnight sleeper trains, the fun to be had in Indian trains (the cheaper the seats, the more interesting the ride), the horrendous 24-hour sleeper bus to Hanoi, the six-hour minibus ride to Phnom Penh with me vomiting most of the way, the slow boat down the Mekong in the pouring rain, the terrifying car drives down mountains in the north of India... They all made the best stories in the end. A flexible and independent itinerary meant that we could add in towns that we heard about from fellow foreigners along the way, places like Jaisalmer, Pushkar and Shimla. Talking to other travellers (as well as locals, of course) was always a joy, whatever their age or nationality.

Mostly, it made us feel young again. We enjoyed the kudos we gained in an instant from younger travellers when we said we were on the road for six months. We couldn't, however, totally align ourselves with backpackers. Because we were approaching our mid-50s, we decided that our backs were not quite up to the challenge. David's camera bag alone weighed 18 kg. Our heads had to rule our hearts and we opted for a medium-size wheeled suitcase each.

Our first aid kit was huge. David knew what the serious stuff should be. His box of tricks included syringes, cannula, scissors, tweezers, scalpel and suture kit which led him to observe that if our budget ever ran out he could probably extract one of my kidneys to sell on the black market. Luckily our financial projections were accurate enough, even if the medical kit was over the top. We used little more than one plaster.

Having visited India as a cash-poor student at the age of 19, I felt I knew that there were only three essentials that I had to pack: diarrhoea-stoppers (a friend kindly gave me a cork as a leaving present), rehydration salts and mosquito repellent. As it turned out, all these would be available along the way. It should be added, however, as every traveller surely discovers, no mosquito repellent actually works. They are the one creature on earth that, as a new vegan, I still have no trouble killing. It's not like mosquitoes are ever going to be endangered and quite honestly it could be a good thing if they were.

When we boarded BA009 to Suvarnabhumi International Airport in Bangkok, I was looking forward to a number of things, the main one being not working. Having worked full-time since 1986, as a journalist in radio and print, I can safely say I felt a little burnt out. We were looking forward to the adventure, the different cultures, religions, spirituality, the people we would meet, the World Heritage sites, the food, the music. We wanted to push our boundaries, feel alive, spontaneous and excited. We wanted to do things that we could bore our grandchildren with for many years to come.

We are not really the kind of people who do beaches or museums but there was a place for them too alongside the diverse mix of countryside, cities, slums, historical sites, ancient temples, volunteering with rescue dogs, stunning beauty and wretched poverty, heat, dust and rubbish. We relished the idea of living out of a suitcase and eating simple food. Many a time we were more than satisfied with fried rice or noodles and a cold beer.

For David, it was all about photography. He armed himself with five cameras, four lenses, lens hoods, chargers, battery packs and remote triggers. In fact, as he casually mentioned as we waited in line for the first airport security check, everything one could possibly need to make a bomb. The quantity of camera gear was something I continued to question long after we had landed in Asia. I was still not sure he had worked out the right storage and cataloguing system for the 25,000 images he was going to take. (To this day, I am not convinced he has it figured out.)

On the day of our departure, he wrote in his journal: 'This journey will, I hope, be a physical, mental and spiritual cleansing. A mid-life re-boot. A time for reflection, taking stock and contemplation of what remains of our all-too-short time on Earth. I hope one day to be an old man in relatively good health, poring over thousands of photos but, as I have witnessed in my job, tomorrow is promised to no one and each day is precious. Hug your dog every day. Tell him he is the best and that you love him totally. Ditto your wife.'

(The dog always comes first.)

Before we left, we knew there were some things that we would not look forward to, and they mainly featured bodily functions. We reckoned that a dose of Delhi belly was inevitable and likely to hit way before Delhi and we hoped that our bladders would hold out on long journeys on public transport.

And the flight home. We were definitely not looking forward to the flight home.

Normally I scroll past YouTube videos on animal rights but for some reason, in the spring before we left home, I clicked on The Food Matrix — 101 Reasons to go Vegan. The speaker was saying that in the United States 300 farm animals die every second.

Every second.

So in the time it takes you to read this sentence, that's about another 1,500 animals slaughtered. And that's just in the US.

I started researching it. I started clicking on more links. No wonder some people call it the animal holocaust. Some people question the use of the word holocaust in this context, but if you take the definition 'destruction or slaughter on a mass scale', which it is, then I don't see the argument. I have no wish to offend Jews or detract from the Holocaust with a capital H.

And it wasn't just the killing of sentient beings that was starting to bother me. It was the unimaginable suffering that comes with intensive factory-farming.

It was quite literally a penny-dropping moment and it was enough to make me vegetarian straight away. But not vegan, as I was keen to tell my sister Nicola, who has been vegan for more than 25 years. 'I could never be vegan.'

She merely replied: 'Never say never.'

꧁꧂

When I mentioned to David that I thought I had had an epiphany, he asked me how many Wet Wipes I was going to need. No, not that, I said. You do realise what we are going to have to do, don't you?

Now, thus far in our lives, we had not been your average tree-hugging, organic, save-the-planet kind of people. We were hard-working parents who had finally, in our 50s, found ourselves with a bit of time on our hands. But when we watched the documentary Dominion as we neared the end of three months in India, we realised we were at a turning point in our lives.

Donald Watson, who founded the Vegan Society in 1944, said that veganism 'starts with vegetarianism and carries it through to its logical conclusion'.

I didn't understand that until 2018. It could be said that I am a fan of the long, slow build-up and certainly our route to vegetarianism had taken its time. We had thought about it before, dabbled a bit, thought we could do it, but we were never really committed. Nothing had given us proper impetus. Not even Nicola's arguments and vegan posts on Facebook. It was only when David suggested being vegetarian, towards the end of 2017, that we decided that we were going to do it. We were doing it for two reasons, partly for our own health. We thought it would be a good idea at our age to cut out red meat, as well as bacon and processed meats. The other reason was that our travels would be taking us to Asia, not exactly known for its animal welfare and quality food production.

David didn't fancy eating meat that turned out to be, say, goat. Personally, that didn't bother me. I didn't want to eat badly kept meat, which could be a potential health hazard. In Kathmandu, a few years back, we had seen slabs of raw chicken out in the sun, unrefrigerated and covered in a layer of dust kicked up by a bus.

The first few weeks of 2018 was easy enough. We didn't want to tell my sister until it stuck. I told her two months later.

What neither of us had anticipated was that our incredible adventure would be life-changing. David and I had managed to take a step back from stressful careers and the pressures of normal family life. Our minds cleared. At last we had the time and emotional energy to read and reflect. It was a journey which time and time again highlighted our concern for people who live in abject poverty, the environment and, above all, animal welfare. This journey would cause us to re-evaluate our place in the world and our relationship with other species.

Ten or 20 years ago, mention of the word vegan might have conjured up an image of a strict, perhaps restricted, diet and militant tree huggers who were a waiter's nightmare but, as we were to discover, veganism is more a way of living that seeks to do the least harm to other living creatures. This, of course, precludes eating animals and fish, but also requires a greater awareness of what happens in the dairy and egg industries, as well as what is in the household products we use, cosmetics, medication and even clothes.

For some, the decision to avoid meat is made on health grounds, for others it is in recognition of the harm that intensive farming inflicts on the environment. For us, it was more about not eating the creatures we claim to love and care about.

Over the coming months, we would talk, discuss and question. It seemed that at every meal-time, we would come up with more questions than answers, more grey areas, more what-ifs. We are reasonable people. What did we think of flexitarians? Was meat reduction enough? Meat only at weekends? Meat-free Mondays? A great start... or akin to saying: 'I beat my wife but only on a Friday'? What would happen to cows if they were no longer used for milking? If farmed animals are no longer forced to procreate, what will naturally happen to them as a species? What would happen if male chicks weren't killed?

As we made our way through India from Madurai in the south to Amritsar in the north, I was surprised by the anger and passion that was firing up inside me. There was no doubt about what we were going to have to do. We were going to have to be vegan.

Ladyboys, lizards and locusts

'The soul is the same in all living creatures, although the body of each is different'

—Hippocrates (460-370 BC)

Since when were choices about what you do on holiday so important? Since the days of social media, that's when. In the past, maybe we would have gone to see a night-time ladyboy show just for fun and maybe we would have visited the long-necked women of the Karen tribe up in the hills. But within our first week in Thailand we found ourselves making judgment calls as to what was an ethical choice and what was responsible tourism.

It's not that we are not open-minded. Perhaps we are too open-minded and are always up for hearing a contrary view. Maybe open-minded is not the right word. I don't want you thinking that we are not up for a bit of fun. David is the most politically incorrect person I know, as well as being someone who loathes injustice, is fascinated by the human condition and is generous to a fault. As is often the case with people who work in the emergency services, he has a dark and, some might say, sometimes inappropriate sense of humour.

He also hates bartering, something that does not necessarily stand him in good stead when it comes to Asia.

I, however, like a bargain and I am not afraid of negotiating a discount off anyone, even if it amounts to 20 pence. Radio interview training with the BBC more than 30 years ago taught me not to have an opinion (I imagine it is quite different now) so I can see both sides on pretty much any subject, which means that I can appear indecisive, which drives David mad. When I do know my own mind on a big issue, however, it does tend to mean that I am on it 110%. As you will see.

So, David and I like a laugh as much as the next person and it surprised us when, so early in our journey, we stopped in our tracks to consider our options. Do we go to a ladyboy show? Is it just a bit of harmless fun for tourists which helps people earn some money for themselves and their families? Or is it tacky, voyeuristic and just another form of exploitation? Does this questioning come with age and experience or social media and social awareness? Do we fear that if we post on Facebook that we went to a ladyboy show, our own friends and acquaintances will judge us somehow?

In reality, deciding factors were the distance from our accommodation in the older part of town, poor reviews online, the cost, and the fact that Lonely Planet, which was always by my side, suggested that to enjoy the nightlife properly, we shouldn't even think about arriving before 11 pm. That's late, we thought. On this one, the practical had outweighed the ethical. And we had decided already that we were going to have to pace ourselves for six months on the road.

Bangkok, the City of Angels, got us off to an incredible start to our adventure. We were indeed going to have to pace ourselves. Not only was it over 30 degrees every day, but also we had to keep to a reasonable budget. That said, we packed in the magnificent Grand Palace and Wat Phra Kaew, Wat Pho and the Reclining Buddha, a tuk-tuk tour at night, the Golden Mount and the inevitable experience of a Thai massage.

I hadn't expected to have to encourage David to do this. I fancied a foot massage, not least because it was so cheap. David opted for a rubdown of his neck and shoulders with a woman who had all the physical charm of a bulldog chewing a wasp and the strength of a sumo wrestler. We were shown to a room where other people were coming in off the street, children, adults, locals, foreigners. David at least got a small booth with curtains around him.

As the woman was seeing only to my feet, I was on one of the many reclining chairs lined up in public. I don't really relax when on full view like that, so it all felt a bit perfunctory. Something to tick off, to say we had had a Thai massage. When in Bangkok and all that.

It wasn't just sightseeing, of course. We had time to wander at our leisure. We enjoyed walking down backpacker street Khao San Road. Twice. The first time, we made the schoolboy error of visiting early in the afternoon, which turned out to be pretty pointless. The time to go was after dark. That's when the place came alive with shops and restaurants, and pubs selling laughing gas and buckets of beer. Here, we had our first sight of takeaway grilled spiders, millipedes and locusts. Would we buy a scorpion on a stick? No, we would not. This was part of the show for the foreign tourist, something for drunken lads on their first trip away from home.

We had read that Rambuttri, which runs behind Khao San Road, had better restaurants, and it did. It was well set up for tourists, but already we were thinking that we were not really tourists. Even though, in all practicality, we were, of course.

We knew that Khao San Road wasn't a true reflection of local life. We were more fascinated by the incredible maze of streets and alleyways of Chinatown, where a map would be useless and where not even tuk-tuks could go. Alleyways got smaller and smaller and there was no end to the number of traders and their tiny shops, stacked to the gunwales with dusty goods, garish plastic toys, thin colourful clothing, jewellery, flip-flops, household goods, all of it cheap and plentiful. How on earth do they all make a living? It was a question I would ask myself pretty much every day for the next six months.

I also wondered what the local traders thought of us, in our funny western clothes, with our white skin, our wealth (even if you are a poor student on a hostelling budget), and how they felt as we looked in on them. Do they wonder why we want to take photos of their everyday life?

Once you have read the book Sapiens: A Brief History of Mankind by Yuval Noah Harari, as we had been doing, you start to question everything you do. Or at least that's what it made us do. And maybe now was the perfect time to be questioning everything.

❧

It was inevitable that sooner or later we would see something distressing. The first such thing was the old white man who had clearly forgotten to catch his flight home 40 years ago and was wearing short shorts, the likes of which you see on 16-year-old girls in Brighton or Benidorm. I suppose we should have counted ourselves lucky that all we could see was his bum cheeks. And not his ancient, pendulous knacker-tackle looking something like the last turkey in the butcher's window, as David put it.

Away from the main tourist streets, we would see cats and dogs in cages, not as many as I thought I might, but enough to make me angry. A young dog stared at us helplessly from behind the bars of a cage. Another looked forlorn attached to a short heavy chain. It was heartbreaking.

Bangkok has a large population of street dogs, or soi dogs as they are known. According to the Soi Dog Foundation (www.soidog.org), there are about 640,000 street dogs in the Bangkok city area. The foundation, which was set up in 2003, is doing great work neutering and vaccinating hundreds of thousands of animals, cats as well as dogs. It aims to provide a humane and sustainable solution to managing the stray population for the health and safety of both humans and dogs.

It also campaigns for better animal welfare across Asia and that includes fighting the dog meat trade. Soi Dog reports that the dog meat trade in Thailand is effectively over but it continues to check for any signs of it coming back and it is now concentrating its efforts on neighbouring countries, particularly places like Vietnam where the trade is alive and well. Or perhaps dead and sick.

On its website, the foundation explains why the dog meat trade must stop: 'The conditions under which dogs are farmed, transported and slaughtered are inhumane and barbaric. The dogs are not humanely killed, many are tortured for hours before being skinned alive. The reason for this is that people believe that the pain inflicted leads to the tenderising of the meat. Most shocking of all is that some dogs are still alive when their fur is removed.'

Although I have been aware that the dog meat trade exists, I had never looked for more information about it, feeling that it was too distressing to think about. But now I firmly believe that we should not pretend it doesn't happen or just cross our fingers that it will go away.

We saw plenty of street cats too and I feared that they had been subjected to some abuse as they had deformed stumpy tails or no tail at all. I was relieved to find out that there is a genetic explanation for this and it is just the way they are.

Thanks to Google, we also looked up all sorts of details about monitor lizards, which we saw from a long-tailed boat ride on the canals. The second largest lizard after the Komodo dragon, an adult monitor can be more than 3 m long and weigh up to 25 kg. These giant, prehistoric-looking lizards lumber along on land with an arrogant swagger, but in the water where they are very much at home, they swim with an elegant grace. The locals don't bother them because they pose no danger to humans and they are seen by many as a sign of good luck and prosperity. The fact that they eat rats, snakes and cockroaches adds to their appeal.

For David, who has always loved reptiles, the monitor lizards were the highlight of the first four days, simply because we hadn't expected to see them. Actually, everything was so photogenic that David thought he had died and gone to heaven. On one occasion he took his time getting a shot of a heron and its reflection. It was only when he viewed the picture on his iPad that he noticed a large monitor lizard casually sitting on a branch above the bird, a cracking shot more by luck than design.

We also loved the simplicity of observing geckos, which came out in the evenings to feast on bugs. They are so cute, with their disproportionately large eyes for night-time vision and hand-like feet. David amused himself by saying 'gecko' every time he saw one, which is fine until you realise that there are thousands of the damn things.

The truly magical moments, the ones which really moved us, were rarely captured on camera or phone. The first happened when we were at Wat Pho at night. Thanks to travelling in the rainy season, there were only half a dozen people there. Gazing up at the temples, we could see the daintiest of rain drops catching the light in the still air, and it was a scene of peace and beauty which will stay with me forever. It was a far cry from the dogs in cages and the cauldron of brown slop being served in the market which really did look like the first day of diarrhoea.

We acclimatised quickly to the heat. The monsoon rain, when it came in the late afternoon, was heavy but it went as quickly as it had arrived. It was too hot even for the lightest throwaway poncho and certainly too hot for the now-ridiculous-looking waterproof trousers we had packed and never came out of the suitcase. When the heavens opened, the easiest thing, we discovered, was to pop in to the nearest bar and have a long iced drink under a fan and watch the world go by.

Yes, we were acclimatising nicely.

Elephants we'll never forget

'Humanity's true moral test, its fundamental test, consists of its attitude towards those who are at its mercy: animals'

—*Milan Kundera, author of The Unbearable Lightness of Being*

I couldn't sleep for a week. From Bangkok we had headed north by sleeper train to Chiang Mai, covering 687 km in 11 hours, to look after rescue dogs at the Elephant Nature Park.

The cacophony of sounds at night kept us awake in our wooden cabin which we shared with two younger volunteers. It started with the cicadas, not just cute cricket chirps from a distant tree, more like a chainsaw in an echo chamber. After rain, the night-time frogs sounded like 1,000 chickens being killed by a fox in the coop.

At night the dogs howled as well as barked. It only took one to start and the wail continued like a Mexican wave all along the run. Some trustworthy dogs who were friendly by day, snoozing on the wooden deck right outside our cabin, became baying wolves at night.

During the day, there was another sound which distinguished this place, that of the pretty girls who started every conversation with 'so' and peppered their every sentence with 'like'. They all emitted the same Americanised twang, regardless of whether they were from Dublin, Sydney, Barcelona or New York. Truth be told, they were lovely, educated young women but we quickly learned that we could get a better conversation if we spoke to them individually. In a pack, the youngsters got ever more dramatic and treated the over-50 as if they were invisible.

Each day we had a routine, poop-scooping, cleaning enclosures, walking and socialising dogs, and putting them in harnesses for a walk in their wheelchairs. Initially we worked with the disabled dogs. They were the most loving souls, all of them physically damaged, but some emotionally too. I particularly loved a black puppy called Marty and a big shaggy dog called Nong Dam. He was a stubborn bugger. And I'll never forget the soft, gentle Khao (pronounced Cow) who bounded up to us full of enthusiasm on the first day. He was a scruffy little thing who often had a nappy on. Most of them dragged their legs behind them, one had no back legs at all, which actually seemed to be a blessing as they were all doubly incontinent and often swished through each other's poo without knowing it. Some had been hit by cars, others had been abused. One was so hurt in his rectum that he was permanently incontinent.

Being a more mature person who has a penchant for questioning things, I dared to ask a member of staff whether a few of these disabled dogs might have been better off had they been put down. One black dog, in particular, struggled to move around, growled at anyone who came too close, and just looked forlorn in his bony, deformed, broken body. I felt his helplessness. The Buddhist culture doesn't allow taking a life, but at what cost to the dog, especially with such limited resources? Anyway, the member of staff certainly disagreed with me, saying that the dogs make remarkable progress. I didn't argue with that and I didn't question the ethos of the place, but I couldn't help but wonder whether it might have been kinder to let some of them go. As far as we were aware, they were not in pain but they had a need for constant care and were often quite grubby and sore. It would be great if they could find a new home but, with their level of need and as 400 able-bodied dogs also lived at the park, it was not likely.

It was humbling to look after these beautiful animals. At the same time it was highly frustrating when walking a stubborn dog who just wouldn't budge, disabled or not. No wonder they dragged their paws – they probably wanted to enjoy their freedom away from their enclosure for as long as they could.

The disabled dogs were particularly vulnerable when they turned over in their wheelchairs. Sometimes they would sniff out a pile of dung from an elephant or a water buffalo and do just what any dog would – roll in it and over they went. This was the epitome of frustration for them, wanting to chase one of the 200 rescued cats at the park or wanting to cock a leg on a tree – and no functioning back legs to do it with. Luckily they didn't poop when walking but they might when putting them in a harness, as David discovered when he got a chicken korma-like splat down his leg when picking up one-eyed Dang for a bath.

It would have been nice if we could have had a bath at the end of the day. In fact, I would have settled for a half-decent warm shower. Facilities were basic, but we were happy to go with the flow, as we reminded ourselves that it was all part of the journey. And we were, after all, still quite fresh. We suspect that we might have had a chance at having a cabin to ourselves but it was bagged, quite rightly, by a young couple who between them were really not well for the whole week. We had a shower which was cold and weak. There were a few bits of string where you could drape clothes to dry and a few nails on the wall to hang your wash-bag. David spent more time wiping down the shower room and washing bugs down the plug-hole than actually showering.

I was grateful for small mercies. At least the large orb spiders stayed outside in their habitat, strung up in their webs between trees. I admit that I wasn't keen on seeing spiders while we were away. I used to be the kind of person who would stamp on a spider if I saw one in my house. I know they are good because they eat flies but nevertheless my natural instinct did not favour our eight-legged friends. It was strange, though, because once I had gone vegetarian, the first time I saw a spider, something (though not a conscious thought) stopped me in my tracks. I fetched a glass and a piece of paper and calmly took it outside. It deserved life.

Although I enjoyed bathing the disabled dogs, I found that it was really quite awkward to be lifting some heavy dogs and putting them into a bowl on the floor while supporting their weight. I didn't want to put my back out. Again, I was annoyed to realise, it was an age-related niggle.

I was at my most content when paddling knee-high in the hydrotherapy pool, encouraging a dog to make another circuit. It was shaded, cool and felt like we were making a real difference to a dog's day, giving them a chance to stretch out their legs and take the weight off their shoulders.

In another area, away from the disabled dogs, we worked with dogs which were quarantined for whatever reason.

My favourite was Dipsy, the only bitch in a lively pack of five in one enclosure. They were playful and friendly, until it was meal-time and then all hell could break loose. She had to be separated as the alpha males were aggressive around food. One breakfast time, I stayed with her in the back room. I sat, leaning against the wall and she made a point of leaving her food to come over to where I was. She leaned in to me and nudged in for a cuddle and a head rub. It was muggy and smelly, I had a huge stain on my bottom from where a dog had tripped me up in a muddy puddle, and I couldn't have been happier. I could have stayed there all day.

The daily dog-walks, of which there were many, took us past most of the 70 rescued elephants at the park. Our focus for the week had been the rescue dogs – but the backdrop to daily life was green hills, water buffalo, and elephants at every turn.

I have a confession to make. David and I have ridden an elephant. Not years and years ago but as recently as four years before our visit to this elephant sanctuary. At the time, it was one of the highlights of our package holiday to India and Nepal, it really was. And yet now, I am horrified that I did it.

Back in 2014, the year when we were celebrating our 50th birthdays, there was a morning when we got up ridiculously early to see the sun rise over the murky mistiness which had descended over Chitwan National Park. We climbed up the rickety steps of a wooden scaffold to reach the elephant's back and we joined another couple on one elephant. Four average adults, about 290 kg between us. We headed off through a shallow river and across grassland and woodland. It was a beautiful experience.

The day before, we had had a talk with a mahout about elephant behaviour. We thought we had asked the right questions. We liked to believe that they were well kept, that the mahouts cared for their animals, and that this was nothing like the elephant tourism in Thailand. We fooled ourselves that, well, if these (already captive) elephants were released back into the wild, they would cause mayhem in the villages. This is what we had been told. And we accepted it. What we didn't ask is how they had been caught in the first place, how they had been trained and why the mahout was carrying a bullhook.

On that same holiday, I sat on the back of an elephant while he showered us with water from his trunk and we all laughed. At that time, David didn't take part in the bathing, not for any ethical reason. He just doesn't like the water. A few others of our group didn't take part, not for any ethical reason that they spoke of, but because they were too old to get their leg over.

Later on, we were taken to a shelter where there were some orphaned elephants. I remember it being the end of another long, hot day and I was not in the mood to be asking questions. I took photographs of a baby elephant in such a way that I cropped out the chain around its ankle.

A couple of years after our India/Nepal holiday, we returned with our adult children for a very special couple of weeks together, on a bespoke tour that we ourselves mapped out. We included the elephant ride and bathing. David sat it out again, because he still didn't like water. I sat it out, because I had done it before and was mindful of saving a few rupees, and… well, actually, I was aware of a growing slightly uneasy feeling about doing it but I don't think I knew why.

Proof of my uneasiness came when I decided not to post the pictures on Facebook. Except for one, where one of the kids was nearly falling off the elephant into the river as he grimly held on like some kind of rodeo – because we thought it was funny.

I'm not laughing now. I can't believe that I was so late to the party on this one. But no one, not even my friends who already knew this, told me specifically about Phajaan. Or maybe they did – and I didn't listen. Phajaan is the barbaric practice of stabbing, beating, even burning elephants, to break their spirit and brutalise them into submission. Every single elephant which is being used for interactions with humans, whether that's riding, swimming, begging, playing music or apparently making art, has had to go through Phajaan. Babies taken from their mothers, mothers killed just for being in the wrong place. The elephant complies with the human's demands – the human armed with a bullhook – only because it is scared of the consequences. An elephant never forgets.

Within hours of arriving at the Elephant Nature Park in Chiang Mai, we were out meeting the elephants and being shown around the grounds by Darrick Thomson, the husband of the park's founder, Sangdeaun Chailert, who is known as Lek. Darrick told us about Phajaan. We were horrified by what we heard. I am not sure how we had been so ignorant, so naive. We were told all about the elephants in their care, elephants that had been beaten, been crippled by years of pulling logs or trekking, or had a life begging on the street or carrying tourists. Here at the sanctuary, at last they can be 'elephant' again, allowed to roam free in beautiful open grounds. The mahouts have been retrained and there are no bullhooks to be seen.

Lek, whose name apparently is Thai for 'small', is a big name in the elephant-saving world. She founded the Save Elephant Foundation and has won many honorary and international awards for her work. Her battle is not easy. The elephant, Thailand's national symbol, has been an icon in the country for centuries.

Volunteers are encouraged to hear her speak on a Thursday evening. The audience included children as young as eight. How I wish I had heard such a message when I was eight, or that my children had. Instead, I was of the generation who would have seen elephants in a circus. Today I can't even bring myself to imagine the training and the transport to get the elephant to a ring in the UK. Anyone who protested at that time was considered a bit wacky. But they were right.

As a child I would have watched Disney's Dumbo without even questioning elephants' presence in a circus. Dumbo was of its time… and then Disney remade it as a live-action version for 2019. At least this time, the movie's director, Tim Burton, made sure that Dumbo was reunited with his mother and they were transferred to a sanctuary.

Of course, on our latest journey through India, we would see quite a few elephants and every single one of them distressed me. The first would be in Madurai. In years gone by, I would have been thrilled to see, at 7 am, walking towards me within the large Meenakshi Temple complex, a decorated elephant with jingling bells. With my new wide-open eyes, I was sad to see such a magnificent beast being imprisoned like this, all in the name of a manmade religion. I wondered what his story was, how boring his life was and how he had been caught and controlled in the first place.

In Alleppey we saw an elephant lying on his side, being washed by three men. When we turned up (an unusual sight of western tourists at the back of a temple off the beaten track), they made sure that they were being kind to him. However well they might look after him was no compensation for the fact that he should not be there in the first place.

And, while we were in Kerala, we took a tuk-tuk south to some smaller town, whose name I forget, where we saw, at the back of a temple, a pitiful elephant, with a chain on his back leg and a rope on the opposite front ankle. He did at least have some shelter from the blazing midday sun. He had a few sugar canes to eat but no water nearby. He was rocking back and forth.

He was the saddest elephant I have ever seen.

Oh ye of little faith

'There is no fundamental difference between man and the higher animals in their mental faculties... The lower animals, like man, manifestly feel pleasure and pain, happiness and misery'

—*Charles Darwin*

At the end of our second week, we had the first test of travelling when things didn't go quite as planned. We had been trying to book a slow boat down the Mekong – not just an hour or so trip, but a method of transport for two days to get us from Chiang Rai across the Thai-Laos border and on to Luang Prabang.

The boat I had read about was really quite charming, if pricey. I hadn't been able to book online so I emailed the company. Although initially I had a swift response, there was a language issue and we waited a few days between replies which ended with the line: 'We don't have a booked [sic] yet.' I took it to mean they didn't have a booking from me. What I later realised they meant was, actually, they didn't have a boat, one of the few drawbacks of travelling in low season.

We headed into the town to find out about other slow boats. I didn't want to opt for a local bus. We went in to the first tour shop we found and signed up pretty fast – the slow boat was the very next day, as per Plan A. But there was no detail of itinerary, no need for passport numbers, no need for contact email or phone number. All we had to do was give one name and the name of where we were staying, and we were given a receipt for money taken. My heart sank when I later noticed that there was no company information on the receipt – neither the slow boat operator nor the tour shop itself. Of course, by the time I noticed, we were too far away to pop back in, if indeed we could ever find it again.

Early the next morning, sitting in the lobby of our guest house, I was anxious and expecting the worst, thinking that we had probably been scammed. If anything can go wrong, it will. I like to think of myself as an optimistic pessimist. My default setting is to fear the worst though I work hard to override this.

They said they'd pick us up at 6.30 am. Remarkably, a van rolled in 15 minutes early. Not only that, but there were eight other passengers. I was mighty relieved. For the two hours it took to drive to Chiang Khong, the driver played music which was probably more appreciated by us than our new young travelmates – Boney M, Blondie and Hot Chocolate.

With a brief stop at a coffee shop with a decent loo, it was 'goodbye Thailand, welcome to Laos'. The minibus driver had been as helpful as he could be, warning us that we should pay no more money anywhere apart from the visa fee. It took us all by surprise just what it took to get as far as the boat – an uncomplicated on-the-spot visa application, followed by a coach, a truck, a stop to buy sandwiches and another truck to get us, finally, to the riverside. Luckily this all passed by very pleasantly as the other passengers were chatty, especially three Americans our age who cheerfully struck up conversations with everyone over the next two days.

We set off on the Mekong mid-morning. Despite the welcome guy warning us that the boat might have to moor up in the event of heavy rain, that didn't happen, even though it rained pretty much non-stop the entire journey. We had an overnight stop in the small town of Pakbeng. Our hotel was about 100 metres from the riverside, which was just as well, as the rain continued to hammer down.

The advice was to get to the boat early on the second day to grab your seat. There was to be no British reserve and the chance of getting the same seat was zero. We were there almost an hour early and we weren't the first. It was a different boat and noticeably less comfortable. Whereas on the first day we had wooden seats with thin cushions, this time we had what looked like seats that had been transplanted from an old minibus and they were not bolted down. The ceiling was patched up and struggling to hold back the leaks. A few buckets were strategically placed on floors and seats. The last person on board had to sit in the wet patch.

David was more worried about the plastic curtains draped down the sides to keep the rain out. He had read about 'death on the Mekong', how adverse currents and a lack of health and safety awareness had contributed to a number of fatalities, and how floating debris can hole a boat in the blink of an eye. He started to wonder how anyone would escape should we have the misfortune to be sinking.

Travellers to Laos, a previously Communist country which opened up for tourism as recently as the early 90s, are advised to beware of scams. On the boat, we saw one playing out right in front of our eyes. A retired British man, now living in Hong Kong, and his companion were asked for their ticket. They explained that they had been asked to hand theirs over the day before – though the rest of us had not. Despite being told they might have to change boat *and* cough up another 210,000 kip (roughly £21), they were remarkably calm about the situation and luckily they had evidence of their tickets on their phone. (I made a mental note to do this whenever we bought a transport ticket for the rest of our journey.) Despite some language barrier and shaking of heads, this was finally accepted.

We had also been warned that, because there are so many noughts on the currency, a common trick (especially by tuk-tuk drivers) is to short-change you by giving back a 2,000 note instead of a 20,000. Mind you, it's silly money. 20,000 kip is worth approximately £1.82.

Talking of tuk-tuks, before we left Thailand, we spent a day with The Tuk-Tuk Club. The cost was more than we had paid for a whole week at the Elephant Nature Park so we hoped it would be worth it. It was.

It was an hour's drive to the Mae Vang area, where we met our guide whose Thai name sounded like City Pong. He was proud to tell us that he was a member of the Karen tribe, which is known for its long-necked women. As we walked up to a hilltop temple, which we had to ourselves, we asked him if he thought a visit to the long-necked women in the hills would be exploitative. He did. We got the impression that it was now something put on for tourists to the point that it is no longer an authentic experience. We decided against it.

We took to tuk-tuks like ducks to water. Our lesson involved learning how to reverse, how to indicate and, importantly, how to brake. We manoeuvred around cones and we did hill-starts. Having passed our admittedly pretty informal tests, we set off into the countryside (luckily nowhere near the city). We visited temples, trundled along tiny lanes, over bridges and past green rice fields. On the itinerary was a visit to a small elephant sanctuary. After a simple but satisfying lunch of egg fried rice and a quarter of a fresh juicy pineapple, we were allowed to feed the elephants sugar cane and we took a bamboo raft downriver. The raft sat quite deep in the water, with a good few centimetres of water swirling around our backsides. I felt safe enough, but I am not sure David did.

'As a general rule of thumb,' he says, 'if you are on a boat and the water is lapping around your goolies, all is not well and there is no room for complacency.'

It was while we were drifting peacefully downstream that we passed an elephant standing in the water. You'll be surprised by what you see when you open your eyes. A couple of young western women in shorts and vest tops were giggling away as the elephant was putting its trunk around them and the mahout was saying: 'Kiss kiss.'

What I noticed (though the girls didn't) was that he was pinching the elephant's ear to make it 'perform'. I wanted to shout at them.

Wherever we went, we were well aware of the huge part played by religion in people's daily lives. In Luang Prabang we got up early for the alms-giving to monks. Less than a minute's walk from our guest house was Wat Nong Sikhounmuang, a small temple that we were told would be less busy than on the main street. I had intended only to watch as a never-ending line of monks passed by in their orange robes. They carried bowls to accept food from the local people, though as far as I could see they only ever got rice. And I suppose they were grateful for it.

I inadvertently offended a woman who was very keen that I sit on a small plastic stool and take from her a bowl of rice. She gestured to me what to do, put a handful of rice in each bowl, and be humble, keeping your eyes cast down. Whatever you do, don't touch the monk. I duly obliged. I felt a bit uncomfortable, the rice was surprisingly hot, having been cooked that morning, and I was conscious about dishing it out with my bare hand. I was starting to wish I was standing on the side of the road taking it all in.

I didn't have much money with me and it turned out she was expecting more than what I initially handed over – but the price had not been agreed beforehand. I paid for the first bowl and gave her the rest of my change but it wasn't enough. Of course she wanted money. I am not sure why I hadn't realised it earlier. This was not a generous gesture on her part, but a way of making a living. She got quite irate, shouting what I can only imagine were Lao expletives, and she slapped her ankle like there was a giant mosquito bothering her.

We packed our swimming gear for our day out at Kuang Si Falls, where there are blissful turquoise pools where people can safely bathe. At least that was what we were expecting. We hadn't factored in the effect of the recent heavy rains. The falls were in full flood and we had to wade through knee-high fast-flowing water even where some of the pathways were.

Thundering downstream, the falls were spectacular, but they were a full-silted murky brown, not picture-postcard turquoise blue, and there was no way anyone was going to risk their life taking a dip. But it was no less beautiful for it. And it was sociable. We bumped into the three Americans from the slow boat and we took each other's photographs, saving us from having to do our own selfies in the spray.

What we also hadn't expected to find was the Tat Kuang Si Bear Rescue Centre at the start of the walk to the falls. The black bears have been rescued from the bile trade.

Hang on. Bile trade. It was all new to me. It turned out to be just as vile as it sounds.

I found it distressing to learn that it used to be common practice to kill bears and remove their gall bladders, bile being a prized ingredient in medical treatments.

More recently, in the 1980s, in places like China and Vietnam, instead of killing the bears, people set up bear bile farms. That meant that bile could be extracted for the duration of a bear's life. The poor animals had to tolerate a life of caged misery, just so that humans could use their bile. According to the organisation Animals Asia (www. animalsasia.org), which has been campaigning to end bear bile farming since 1998, there are still more than 12,000 bears on bear bile farms. And, they add, most farmed bears are starved, dehydrated and suffer from multiple diseases and malignant tumours that ultimately kill them.

It is always the figures I find astonishing.

12,000 bears.

Picture just one, kept in a tiny cage. It will have a hole in its gall bladder so the bile can be extracted or it might have a permanent catheter. That bear which has grown into its cage, its body contorted to fit the bars. It may even have lost its teeth from trying to bite its way out. How on earth did someone first discover that bile belonging to bears might be considered good for humans? It made me sad, it made me angry, it made me feel helpless, it kept me awake at night.

At the entrance to the falls, humans were invited to sit in a cage to see for themselves how uncomfortable it would be to sit there for five minutes, let alone a lifetime. The sign read: 'If you don't want to spend ten years in here, what makes you think bears do?'

What's the worst that can happen?

'We all love animals. Why do we call some "pets" and others "dinner"?'

—*Singer k.d. lang*

'It'll be fun,' he said. 'It'll be part of the adventure. We have loads of time and we can see more countryside on the way.'

David's suggestion? Take the 24-hour bus to Hanoi instead of a one-hour flight. Many months before we left home I had done my research and concluded that a flight was the way to cover the distance. But I capitulated, not wanting David to think I didn't have a sense of adventure and an ability to go 'off plan'. And to be honest I had forgotten, for now, the description of the 'journey from hell'.

The night before, David couldn't sleep because of three Cokes and two Americanos. I couldn't sleep because I was worried that there would be only one driver for 24 hours.

We set off from Luang Prabang at 6 pm in a dirty old bus full of garish flashing lights and raucous Asian music. An hour later, all was quiet and dark. Everyone settled in to sleep in their reclining seats. Actually, they were locked in the reclining position. This was our lot for 24 hours.

Surprisingly, at least for the first few hours, it was rather comfortable, if claustrophobic. We had found out only after we had booked the ticket that there was no toilet on board. We had been lulled into a false sense of security when we had used the Green VIP Bus from Chiang Mai which was super-comfortable, air-conditioned, had a toilet on board, and we were even given a bottle of water and a biscuit. Nothing like that here.

'Driver will stop for you,' we were told. He did. The first time was in the pitch black, in pouring rain, at the side of the road. I squatted behind the bus and will be forever grateful I didn't have the squits. Indeed, since you ask, after taking three Imodium as a preventative measure earlier in the week, I was well bunged up. What a blessing.

David jumped out to pee, but he was left standing between the bus and a perilous ditch. The young men, he said, peed like racehorses within seconds and jumped back on the bus, leaving him trickling away with his 50-something bladder. There he was, trying to piss in the pissing rain, conscious of the old adage: 'More than three shakes is a wank.'

Back in the bus, my wet T-shirt made me shiver under the air-con. Luckily we were given blankets. The bus stopped occasionally to drop off or pick up parcels and people, many of whom slept on the floor down the central aisle. Suddenly we were aware that there was a baby on board, probably only a matter of two weeks old. Fortunately, she slept most of the way. At 6 am, music and lights came on. 'Did you order a wake-up call?' David asked.

We reached the Laos-Vietnam border at 6.15 and waited for the crossing to open at 7. And that's when the fun really began. The officials did not like that our in-principle visa permission stated that we would arrive at Hanoi Airport. There seemed to be some suggestion that we'd have to go there. David worried that we'd be sent back to Luang Prabang. I worried that the bus had left without us, as everyone else had already cleared immigration and they were nowhere in sight. This concern was only slightly tempered by the fact that we had our suitcases with us as everything had to go through a scanner.

It would appear that the Vietnamese border staff, much like border staff the world over, have their sense of humour removed before joining the service. The more senior they are, the more stripes they have on their shoulder and the more self-important they become. I hovered near a counter, keen that they wouldn't forget us. More than once, I was ordered in no uncertain terms to go and sit down.

About an hour later, after much to and fro and us filling in forms we had already filled in, we were allowed to rejoin our fellow passengers, though we still didn't have our passports in hand. By now the bus was 500 metres away up a hill as the driver had used the time to get petrol, but I was just happy to see it. I got on the bus, stressed, shrugging my shoulders apologetically to fellow passengers who seemed to have more patience than I would have in that situation. David waited outside until our passports arrived.

After an eternity, a man on a motorbike pulled up and from inside his jacket produced our passports which he then decided required one last examination. His patience worn thin, David snatched them away, swore under his breath and got back on the bus.

The journey continued. The lunch stop was at a 'very local' roadside café where heaps of rice were being served with clear soup and some unidentifiable meat. But it was the smell of festering botulism that made us cross the road for a packet of crisps. In his ambulance career, David has smelled some pretty nasty niffs, but this was up there with the worst of them.

After lunch the road got smoother. We were now on straighter roads so there was less sideways motion to the bus. But it got hot. Stiflingly hot. The air-con was a small puff of air you could just feel if you put your hand up to it. Fortunately more people were getting off so that, and an increasing cloud cover, helped. I had also been heartened to see that there were two or three drivers taking turns at the wheel.

We were just thinking our journey was nearing an end when we and half a dozen others were told to get off the bus. We were at the side of a busy road and we were put on another passing coach. No explanation was given but luckily (this is starting to read like a game of 'Fortunately, Unfortunately') I had read on a blog that this sometimes happens. The seats in the new bus at least allowed us to sit up properly. There was even a TV screen showing a Vietnamese farce, a cross between Monty Python and Benny Hill. Not that it kept us amused. That cloud cover became a thunderous downpour with spectacular lightning. Now I feared a dreadful road accident on treacherous dark, flooded roads.

We didn't reach the bus station in Hanoi until 8 pm, a full 26 hours later. We were immediately surrounded by taxi drivers and various other hangers-on. Talk about intimidating. We had been told to expect a taxi fare of 20-30,000 dong and they were asking 150,000. We settled on 50,000 with a man who kept flashing a 100,000 note. He failed to drop us off at the right address and when we handed over 50,000 dong he started shouting and gesticulating. It turned out that he thought he was getting 100. It was the old trick of trying to take tourists for a ride by saying the agreed fare was 50 *per person*.

While he hollered, we walked away. We hadn't a clue where we were and no idea which way to turn. An old man realised that we were having problems and although he couldn't speak English, he knew someone who could and he led us to a charming Australian who ran the Pirates Den. In his pub, Chris called up a map and, better still, allowed me to use his loo. I also used his wifi to let our Airbnb host know that we were in the area. (24 hours later, we would go back to buy Chris a beer.)

We started walking down the street as directed. Minutes later, it was quite surreal when a young man on a motorbike pulled up and asked me if I was Caroline. Our host had found us and he led us the final 100 metres to our accommodation. To top it all, we were on the fourth floor. With David's heavy suitcase. Without a lift. Of course we were.

And that is how we arrived in Hanoi, sweaty, unwashed for 26 hours, teeth and hair unbrushed, hungry and jaded but alive and safe with a tale to tell.

And to think we could have taken a plane in an hour.

Hanoi, the capital of Vietnam, left an impression on us, in no small measure due to the location of our Airbnb just outside the Old Quarter. Entry and exit was via padlocked shuttered doors. From the hallway you could borrow a Vietnamese hat, an umbrella and a motorbike.

As soon as we stepped outside, the heat hit us. The street was already alive — it had been since dawn. Women selling fresh meat, chickens in a basket, a few fish in a tin bowl.

One man was selling baked sweet potatoes, which looked like they had been there a while. Occasionally a fresh batch came out and we wondered if he ever sold all that he baked. Fruit sellers set down bowls which were attached to their shoulder poles. You can only imagine the weight as women walked down the street, getting in to some kind of rhythm and looking like they couldn't quite stop until they reached their destination.

All kinds of fresh fruit, and I mean fresh, not packaged in plastic, but the juiciest tastiest mango, watermelon and pineapple and plenty other fruit that we don't get at home — longan, mangosteen, dragonfruit. Mobile street sellers pushing carts or riding bicycles had little loudspeakers advertising their wares. In our residential district, we walked past open doorways at all times of the day. Life, it seemed, was very much out on the street. It is very much a community. We were assured it was safe — and it felt it too.

As we walked to the Pirates Den for a beer one Saturday evening, about 7 pm, everyone's doors were open, families had gathered together for a meal, as many as a dozen sitting on the floor of a small room, sharing the food. The church was holding a service, the congregation spilled outside, everyone young and old sitting on small plastic stools on both sides of the narrow street, allowing just enough room for motorbikes to get through.

Apart from the Aussie who ran the Pirates Den, we seemed to be the only western people 'this' side of the highway which divided us from the Old Quarter, a mere ten-minute walk away.

We were told that the Vietnamese work seven days a week, they eat eight times a day, go to the market three times a day. They get up early and go to bed late. A fruit seller might go the wholesale market at 2 am, ready to sell at 6 and she might still be away from home until 9 pm if sales are slow. All shopkeepers seem to expect slow sales. They sit around chatting outside their narrow store or lie down on anything for a siesta. Outside most shops, apart from a lot of parked motorbikes blocking the pavement, are small red and blue plastic stools for adults to sit on.

The traffic is crazy. There are about five million motorbikes in the city. They are supposed to drive on the right, but crossing any street you have to expect a motorbike to come from any direction on any side of the road. We saw everything possible carried on a motorbike — a family of four with young children, a babe in arms, dogs, giant panes of glass, scaffolding poles, large boxes of goods, huge plastic bottles, a grandmother with a bunch of flowers. Most motorcyclists don't wear helmets and many are on their phones. But they either slow down slightly for a pedestrian, particularly a western one, or they will go around you. The pedestrian cannot assume that a zebra crossing means they're any safer. All you have to do is observe the traffic, to see if there is a slight break in it, pick your moment and go for it — confidently. No hesitation. If worried, you keep walking and put your hand up slightly as if to say: 'Thank you very much, I am crossing here.'

A new hazard came later in Ho Chi Minh City, where motorcyclists jump the traffic by going up on the pavements. We had no near-misses and we saw no road rage. That said, it was in the back of our minds that on average one person is killed on Vietnam's roads every hour and it's usually a motorcyclist. In Hoi An, we met two young women from London who had matching burns on the inside of their ankles. It turned out that they had been passengers on a motorbike and their ankles had been resting on the exhaust for a matter of only five minutes. They didn't notice it

happen but when they got off the bike a layer of skin came away. They learned that there is a name for it — the Asian tattoo.

In reality, probably the most dangerous moment was on an overnight train from Danang to Ho Chi Minh City. Early in the morning, before everyone was awake, David decided that he needed to clamber down from his upstairs bunk to go for a pee (old man's bladder and all that). Now, he has all the elegance of Boris Johnson in a tutu, and instead of grabbing a fixed piece of metal rail, he leaned on the flimsy curtain pole above my bunk, which was never going to hold his weight. He went flying (skydiving as he would have it), and there was a thud and a clatter as he landed and the pole crashed down on top of me. Just as I had started to doze. He did the British thing of swiftly standing up, brushing himself down, bidding me good morning and hurrying off to the loo. Not surprisingly, I didn't get back to sleep, not least because I was now exposed to anyone who walked by.

It was while we were in Hanoi that we became aware of different food items that were available. I went as far as looking up how we could say 'no meat' in Vietnamese. *Không thịt*. We sat in restaurants where there was tortoise on the menu. Most of Vietnam's 25 species of tortoise and turtle are threatened due to the illegal trade for meat, the international pet market or for traditional medicine.

We have tortoises at home. They are wondrous, gentle creatures. We certainly couldn't imagine eating them. I mean, why would you?

In the back streets, we saw bodies of small- to medium-sized dogs which had been spit-roasted whole. I looked away as soon as I had realised what they were. I shared on Facebook the information about what we had seen and there was horror. Quite a reaction. It was my sister who commented: 'What's the difference?'

What's the difference between tortoise on the menu in Vietnam and crab or lobster on the menu at home? What is the difference between a spit-roast dog in Hanoi and a hog roast at a summer party in Jersey?

For the first time I found myself admitting, there is no difference.

I now know that the last time I ate meat was in Hoi An. When we travel, I like to choose where to eat by consulting TripAdvisor and I had read of a place that was getting five stars. We found the restaurant easily, tucked away behind a main street. I was still faffing putting my bag under the table when waiters came over with food. I hesitated and asked if there was a menu but there was no such thing. Everyone got the same — the house speciality of meat, salad and a giant pancake to wrap it in. We looked at each other and, in a typically modest British reserve not to make a fuss, or to offend, decided to stay put and eat it.

We made a pact that we would not tell my sister. We didn't actually enjoy it. I realised that I did not miss meat at all.

We had had a similar experience a week or so earlier in Old Hanoi. The Australian publican had recommended a new restaurant around the corner. It was not a road we would otherwise have ventured down, but he said it was safe, even after dark. What we found was a buzzing little place, open-plan, with rows of tables, and a particularly young crowd, all the more joyful for the fact that there were no other tourists.

Again, there was really only one option. Everyone got the same — a plate of raw meat to cook on a table-top barbecue in front of you. The concept of sociable eating was fun and we were supporting a new business, not an international chain. Again, we felt committed and ate it anyway. There were different kinds of meat, all of them unidentifiable, some of them marinated in bright reds and oranges.

I'm glad we did it, for it was part of the journey, nudging us further to the realisation that we had no need for this in our lives and coming away with a stronger resolve.

It's strange because, up until December 2017, I ate anything and everything. I had no problem (another thing I am ashamed to admit) sampling foie gras on a taster menu at a smart hotel; I have eaten barbecued goat in Zambia; I would have veal schnitzel in Austria; I did at least try oysters once though I think they are the worst thing in the world. How often do we think we enjoy seafood, when really we are only enjoying whatever sauce it is covered in? Can you imagine eating a plate of naked, unflavoured mussels? *Moules* without the *marinière*. The only way they are palatable is with a creamy wine sauce and I reckon maybe the gimmick of using a shell as a tool was introduced to distract you from what they're really like.

Anyway, while we were in Hanoi, we went on a walking food tour, just the two of us and our guide. We pointed out that we were vegetarian but admitted that we were new to it and so it wouldn't be the end of the world if we slipped up. That was our mistake.

We had a fabulous morning exploring alleyways that we would never have otherwise found. As usual, it was hot, sweaty and exciting. We were even tempted to try some crab in a market. I worried more about getting food poisoning than sticking to my morals.

And then we were taken to a stall where an old woman was sitting in front of a bubbling vat of oil. She had some patties which looked like pale burgers and our guide invited us to taste them before guessing what they might contain. When it involves guesswork, you kind of know it'll be something unusual. It had been fried twice, once in preparation, and again in front of us to heat it through. It wasn't particularly tasty or memorable, other than the fact that it turned out to be worm. Great.

And then he kissed us

'You may never know what results come of your
action, but if you do nothing there will be no result'
                                        —Mahatma Gandhi

If Vietnam gave us our first uneasiness about food, it also
gave us our first uneasiness about what we are doing to our
planet.

Halong Bay is on everyone's list of places to visit if you
are anywhere near the north of Vietnam. It is truly magnificent and far bigger than I imagined. We booked a mini-
package to be picked up from Hanoi and dropped back
there, which was a great idea if only because it meant we
could leave a suitcase behind and travel relatively light. One
night on board a boat in the bay and two nights on Cat Ba
Island sounded like a delightful mini-break within our independent travel plans.

Our boat mates were a Korean honeymoon couple who
could hardly speak English, though we tried our best to
communicate, and half a dozen Egyptian 30-somethings
who were obviously on a laddish break and they barely even
looked in our direction.

On the first night we moored up, the weather was sultry and we were lucky enough to see the sun set, despite it being cloudy for most of the day. At 1 am, it sounded like we were being hit by cannon fire. The storm was right overhead and the thunder seemed to ricochet around the limestone islets. We actually felt the noise drumming through the wooden boat. We were only slightly reassured by the fact that there were dozens of other boats moored near us.

The next day we enjoyed visiting a cave, climbing lots of steps for fabulous views, and we cooled off by swimming from a manmade beach. Our favourite bit was hopping into kayaks to head off through a low natural arch into a lagoon. Although David is not entirely relaxed on the water, he will sit on board something that gives him buoyancy. We were sure it wouldn't be as bad as the first time we kayaked together. We had met only a few weeks before and David felt the need to show off. We set off from a beach on the north coast of Jersey with our guide telling us: 'Only a fool can capsize one of these.' Challenge duly accepted. Just as we got way out of our depth and beyond the reach of the beach, over he went. He was utterly terrified and thought he would drown. I was annoyed that I didn't have my camera to hand and was more concerned that his designer sunglasses had gone overboard. (I rib him mercilessly about many things but David has a reason for his dread of water. His older brothers once tried to drown him.)

So, this lagoon in Halong Bay. Sounds idyllic. Well, it was beautiful in its own right. Peaceful, beautiful greens and blues, though no birds and no wildlife that we could detect. But the plastic. Oh the plastic. I started pulling plastic bottles, crisp packets and carrier bags out of the water. It was the least I could do but it wasn't enough. And yet it wouldn't take much to keep on top of it. Why oh why can't staff members from the thousands of boats that go out there every year not keep on top of it, maybe invest in a net or two, to trawl around and keep it clean? Is it too much to ask?

The next stage of our mini-break was to get to Cat Ba Island. I had envisaged a small, remote island with clean beaches and crystal clear water, a place where we would lie on a beach and read a book and feel like we were a world away from it all.

We transferred back to the harbour, took a short taxi ride, and (something we weren't expecting) the guide then left us to sort ourselves out for the rest of the time. We had no voucher, no proof of who we were and I was concerned that the hotel would not have heard of us. We were assured all was booked and they were expecting us. We were shown to a speedboat to whizz across the bay to Cat Ba Island. We headed off at speed, as per the boat's job description, wind in our hair, looking at each other excitedly as the adrenaline flowed.

And then, just as we were in the middle of nowhere, the engine cut out. We laughed and said pleasantries to the skipper. After a while, we realised he really didn't know what to do.

Ever helpful, David said: 'Ask the audience or phone a friend?'

Luckily the skipper had his mobile phone and he phoned a friend. We were a good ten minutes floating in silence — he didn't have an anchor or anything to prevent us drifting.

Where were all the tourist boats when you needed them? They had all gone back to harbour for a changeover of guests. Before long, another boat from the island was heading our way. Its driver stopped to ask if we were ok and he said someone would be along soon. What we ended up doing was transferring into another boat. We had to hop over in the middle of the bay, bobbing up and down, as well as lug across a large suitcase, two rucksacks and David's cameras. I am not entirely sure what happened to the man in the broken-down boat but I hope he got home eventually.

First impressions of Cat Ba Island were not good. Where we landed was like an abandoned building site. We caught a bus and we drove for half an hour before we reached the main town. I had no idea the island was big enough for a bus, let alone a half-hour drive.

On the last day, our activity involved climbing up a mountain in the rainforest in the National Park in the hope of bumping into one or two of their golden-headed langurs. Not that it was likely. There are about 70 langurs in an area twice the size of Jersey.

A conservation programme to save the golden-headed langur is surely too little too late. The local population has already eaten the rest. But we reckoned that if anyone could find a langur, it was our guide, who was introduced as Monkey Man.

The first ten minutes in the park did not impress. The litter was a problem. There was a monkey in a cage. A sign said it was a temporary rescue place. I was not so sure. Apparently this National Park is home to 32 types of mammal and 70 bird species. We saw three or four deer. We heard frogs croaking. (It had been beautifully wet for them.) We walked through what looked like an abandoned homestay area with a pool. It had seen better days. The guide insisted it was a good photo opportunity. David obliged. It was easier than questioning it. Then Monkey Man grabbed a crab and tried positioning it for a photo. The crab scuttled off and fell unharmed off a tree.

This happened a few times as the guide tried to reposition it. It's ok, we said, let's leave it. I was glad when eventually the crab won the day by hiding around the back of a tree where he couldn't be disturbed.

Then we saw two huge spiders. I hoped to God the guide was not going to pick them up. David's camera struggled with the humidity and he had to keep wiping the lens. We didn't get the spider photo.

It was quite a climb up, with manmade steps through the forest. Although the park had some strategically placed bins they were all full and there were other piles of rubbish elsewhere, especially plastic bottles. It never ceases to amaze me how people can't be arsed to carry an empty plastic bottle back down a hill. Surely most of the visitors should be interested in ecotourism, something Cat Ba is trying to champion.

In terms of experiencing a rainforest it was worth doing. It was, inevitably, humid and sweaty and we had close encounters with mosquitoes and other assorted biting bugs. The guide gave us sturdy sticks. To stave off snakes, we guessed. It turned out that they were more trek pole than self-defence weapon. On the final ascent we put down the sticks so that we had both hands free in order to clamber up the rocks.

At the very top there was a lookout shelter, though there was not much to look out for as it was all green forest and mist. It was nevertheless an accomplishment and the cool breeze was welcome. Monkey Man had a fag in the fresh air and checked Facebook on his phone while we took photos. Then he made odd noises as if to summon some monkeys for us. Nothing happened. I mean, why would a monkey with 160 km of forest to explore come to an area littered with plastic bottles, a local in a Man United T-shirt and two sweaty tourists? A thought flitted through my mind. Unless there was food…

No, luckily he didn't entice the wildlife with food, but he made more silly sounds cupping his hands and blowing through rolled leaves. He put one leafy frond to his chin. 'Ho Chi Minh,' he said drily.

His sense of humour now coming to the fore, he gestured to me to sit next to him on a wooden railing. He had been directing us for photos all the way so I assumed he was doing it again. There was a precarious drop behind.

'Don't do it if you're not comfortable,' David warned. I recognised that this was his understated way of saying: 'Fuck that.'

Having mentally done a quick risk assessment, I sat as I was told, not feeling it was too dangerous. Before I knew it, Ho Chi Minh jumped up on a slippery wet post and balanced on one leg, his arms outstretched. Now that was dangerous. We had ourselves a performing monkey after all.

Back at the bottom we bought him a cold drink. We gave him a $5 tip and in return he gave David a smoky, sweaty hug as well as a kiss on the back of his neck, which we laughed about all the way back to the town.

There's a family friend of ours who is in his 90s who had warned us about monkeys on the menu in places like Vietnam. He enjoys nothing more than recalling his travelling days in Asia, the days well before mobile phones and social media. The days when foreign travel truly meant being away from, and out of touch with, home. He had personally witnessed monkey being served in a restaurant, not just prepared as a steak, but something way more horrific.

It is considered a delicacy for a live monkey, chained to the table, to have its head sliced open right in front of diners so that they can then scoop out the fleshy brain, as fresh as it comes. Thankfully we didn't see anything like it, nor did we see restaurants where it might still exist today. If we had, I think I would have vomited on the table.

It is when I hear of such ludicrous practices that I wonder whether we should all boycott these countries and not even set foot in them. Would it make a difference? Do we have the right to challenge other people's traditions and cultures? Too bloody right we do. It is our responsibility to speak up for those who have no voice.

It was during our time away that I took to signing e-petitions against animal cruelty worldwide, something I had never done before. I hope they make a difference. Such practices are so disgusting, so barbaric, unnecessary and sickening and it makes me feel so helpless that I want to cry again.

We were in Cat Ba Town for only 24 hours, with no time or inclination to go off in search of sporty activities. This is an island which, according to Lonely Planet, is emerging as northern Vietnam's adventure-sport and ecotourism mecca. My trusty book also warned that Cat Ba Town has experienced a hotel boom, with a chain of ugly concrete hotels springing up. There was nothing of note in the town. It was scruffy and we couldn't tell if buildings were going up or falling down.

We walked around the coast to a beach which was unimaginatively named Cat Ba 1. Plenty of people were cooling off in the sea, but right behind the beach was a huge building site. Construction of a new luxury beach resort had started.

The best part of the day was finding our hotel's rooftop bar and pool. We had the pool to ourselves, just how I like it. From up here we could appreciate the view of local fishing boats and floating seafood restaurants (nice view, not so good for the fish), but we could also see evidence of their lack of planning policies. Who allowed that building to block up the view between two hills, hills that were as impressive as Halong Bay's own islets? Who allowed that new hotel to be so high?

On our last day, sitting on a street corner waiting for the bus, we reflected that we had been sad to leave some places on our journey. Not so characterless Cat Ba Island.

Our journey continued south via Hué and Hoi An. We spent a night in Danang in order to catch the train to Ho Chi Minh City (I prefer the name Saigon which many Vietnamese still use). It was a little difficult getting the train booked and I was worried that we would be in the cheap seats, which wouldn't be much fun for a 17-hour journey.

'What's the worst that could happen?' was a phrase we were well used to asking ourselves. Once we were in the cabin, which had four berths and not six as had been suggested at one point, my worst fear was that my back would seize up, and we were glad that we had opted for suitcases and not backpacks. We reflected on a blog about the difference between backpackers and tourists. We liked to think that at our age we were a hybrid of both. I felt guilty if I didn't eat the local food but sometimes chips or pizza could be a lifesaver. It was also a matter of embracing the aces and observing the good and the bad without wishing it were any different or imposing our views or standards. Except when it comes to animal welfare, of course.

We also liked the fact that not everyone spoke English. We didn't expect all street signs and café menus to be in our language — and they often weren't. A bit of difficulty communicating was part of the fun. We came across a Cao Dai temple in Danang. It's not a religion that I was familiar with. Adherents worship a diverse combination of saints including Julius Caesar, Joan of Arc and Victor Hugo. We met a lovely young woman who didn't speak much English but she whipped out her iPhone and tapped out a few sentences on Google Translate. It doesn't quite replicate conversation but we did learn that followers lead a life of non-violence and vegetarianism.

Travelling is so much more than just seeing sights. It's about who you meet along the way. I recall Michael Palin saying much the same thing many years ago. Long after the photos of temples and beaches have faded, it's the people (and animals) we will remember. Vietnam had given us our three best characters so far — Monkey Man, Thang and Sexy Lady.

Thang was the owner of our guest house in Hué. It looked like he may have been electrocuted as his long wild blond hair was sticking out all over the place. He was perhaps stuck in the 60s and might still smoke something from that era. When we came back to the guest house after a day exploring, he showed off his scrawny seven-year-old chicken. He picked up a homemade paper sign and hung it around the chicken's neck. 'Fuck KFC,' it read.

Sexy Lady looked harmless enough when we met her. She guided us to the river where we were to try steering a small coracle made from bamboo and cow dung. On the short walk a few of us were bothered by insects flitting around our necks and ears. We batted them away. I thought I had something like a large butterfly stuck under the rim of my hat. It turned out that Sexy Lady was the joker of the pack, tickling us all from behind with a soft leafy sheaf of something.

That was nothing compared to what was coming. She showed us how to get in the boat, standing on one leg, spinning in a circle and then dancing and singing to the tune of Gangnam Style. She would take away a paddle, or hold the boat from behind so you could paddle as much as you liked but you would get nowhere, she would jump in the boat with you or transfer between two in the middle of the river, which she called the 'happy water'. She seemed to have a different trick for each person who got in a boat. All effortlessly done and all very amusing.

She was 66. Priceless.

I was moved to tears when I least expected it. Sometimes it was simply the joy of travel. Sometimes I thought it was Menopausal Woman at work. I mean, how do you know if you're having a hot flush when you seem to be having exactly that from the minute you get up to the minute you go to bed because it's hot and humid the whole time? It turned out that travel was a great antidote to most menopausal symptoms. We were so busy and seeing so much that was new and exciting and challenging that I didn't stop to think about how I was feeling... other than hot and sweaty. Any minor niggles I might have had at the start now seemed insignificant when compared to the challenges that people in Asia, particularly women, face on a daily basis.

Quite bizarrely, I felt emotional on the train to Ho Chi Minh City. My fears that the train compartment would be too hot, cramped and claustrophobic were unfounded. It was air-conditioned to the point of being cold, but I had a clean blanket as well as my scarf for my shoulders so I was happy. The other potential hazard was always the toilet, but it was clean, stocked with toilet paper and kept fresh with the window open. The door lock was broken but I could work around that.

It was 3 pm and the journey was flying by. I had already updated my diary, written a blog post, read my book and dozed off. Some people like reading a book by a pool. I discovered that I like reading a book on a train. I impressed myself with my ability to go with the flow of the journey, rather than feel impatient or bored. David's words about travelling distances had stayed with me and I decided this was a good thing for me to observe. Be in the moment, be present, don't be too anxious about reaching your destination on time. It didn't necessarily come easily for me, so it was as good a time as any to be mindful.

My mind had not been on the movement of the train or my environment, other than to delight in it. I took the chance to stretch my legs and I stood in the corridor to watch the world go by. I welled up just by freezing a moment in time to take in what I was seeing while letting it sink in that we were actually doing this, we were actually travelling, we had got out of the rat race, off the treadmill, away from the daily grind...

We moved out of a small station. We passed open green paddy fields — such bright light green; occasionally one person in the middle of the field, wearing the ubiquitous conical Vietnamese hat; rows of tall palm trees; houses built in rectangular shapes, shaded open area at the front, washing hanging out, a parked motorbike or three; many ramshackle areas but also some lovely properties; quite randomly a small cemetery, with colourful square-shaped memorials; some hazy low hills in the background breaking up an otherwise flat vista; a lone brown cow (we didn't think it could be a Jersey as its neck was too baggy); water buffalo — the simple delight of seeing a small water buffalo calf in a wet field.

In our cabin, initially I was feeling a bit hard done by as the woman in the lower berth immediately shut the curtains, turned over and went to sleep, even though it was still daylight. It was like we all had to respect that, but I really wanted to peep out of the window. The curtains stayed closed even though her husband and the child they were with, probably their grand-daughter, were now all wide awake. They were friendly enough, even if they spoke no English.

And then there were the people who did want to speak to us, just to practise their English. I had had a lovely chat with a sweet young student at the railway station. She was returning home to her village after being in Danang to take her younger brother to hospital after a motorbike accident — he had one arm in plaster, the other was heavily bandaged. Her clothes were quirky and modern, and she was wearing her orange motorbike helmet, I presume because she couldn't be bothered to carry it. I was going to ask but we had so many more interesting things to talk about and before I knew it she was off to catch her train.

I returned to the cabin because Mango Man needed to pass by with his trolley of eggs, fresh mango and bananas. Such healthier snacks than Mars bars and cheese and onion crisps. He had a deep resonant voice as he called out 'mango' or something in Vietnamese as he walked down the corridor.

We were hoping that trains in India would be this good.

It's not very autism-friendly, is it?

'If you haven't any charity in your heart,
You have the worst kind of heart trouble'

—*Bob Hope*

Frequently, as we made our way south from Hanoi to Hoi An to Ho Chi Minh City, we found ourselves observing: 'It's not very autism-friendly, is it?' Nowhere was this more obvious than on a visit to the Cu Chi Tunnels. The extensive network of tunnels were built for the Viet Cong to have a fighting chance against the Americans in their 20-year war, which finally ended in 1975.

It's a strange mix of tourism meets history. The booby traps are brutal. You can lower yourself into a hole for a quick photo. You can go underground and crawl on your hands and knees through a few of the tunnels. I was surprised that I couldn't bring myself to do it. One grandmother from South Africa was braver than I was, but she went so slowly that she lost sight of the person in front of her and so missed a turning. The uniformed man in green who had taken up the rear emerged without her.

When the rest of her family realised that she hadn't surfaced, a member of staff had to go looking for her and she had to reverse on hands and knees out of the tight tunnel, which by all accounts was really quite awkward. She was quite shaky when she surfaced. As we were preparing to head back into Ho Chi Minh City, she realised that she had dropped her phone in the tunnel and someone had to go back and fetch it. I imagine the experience gave her nightmares. (Getting stuck, not dropping her phone.)

Also at the site, tourists can have a go firing AK-47s. The noise was horrendous and I felt that it was somewhat inappropriate to be glorifying guns in a place that remembers such a pointless war. While we had an ice cream, we thought of all the people we know who are on the autism spectrum. Not one of them would have liked the noise. There was a time when my own son would have had a meltdown with such a racket. When we all went to Varanasi in the east of India, as a family in 2016, the only time that I consciously considered his autism was when we went to the night-time Aarti ceremony on the River Ganges. Every night, it's a blast of chanting, music, jangling and smoke. Combine it with the hooting of the motorbikes and the chaos of the jammed traffic on the way there, the thousands of people and the stuffy heat, and you have all the ingredients for sensory overload.

A meltdown, to Seb, was a silent retreat, a withdrawal and a need to move away. He just managed to cope to the end of the ceremony and then we caught our cycle rickshaws back to the hotel, where he skipped the evening meal and curled himself up in the foetal position for the night.

After the tunnels, we returned to Ho Chi Minh City via a workshop supporting disabled people affected by Agent Orange. We had learned more about the deadly chemical at the War Remnants Museum, where there were emotive displays about what they term the American War. To be honest, all I really know of the war is from movies like Platoon, Full Metal Jacket and Good Morning, Vietnam.

As a journalist of 30-odd years, I was moved reading about war photographers who had died in action, people like Larry Burrows and Henri Huet, fascinated by the power of the monochrome images, and interested to read of women like Catherine Leroy and Dickey Chapelle who had also been documenting the war.

I was disturbed to read about war crimes committed by the Americans. Thousands of children have been born with genetic defects because the Americans sprayed poisonous chemicals over the jungle areas to destroy the Vietnamese military's cover. The dioxin was one of the deadliest chemicals ever manufactured. Soldiers who came into contact with it found that their ears bled. Their children have been born with horrendous defects, cleft palates, blindness and paralysis.

The legacy of the futile war goes on.

We were enjoying the company of four of our fellow minibus passengers so much that we decided to have a late lunch together. Over another bowl of egg fried rice and dosa, we put the world to rights. The conversation distracted us from the painfully slow service and the large rat which scurried along a shelf on the wall.

It was a busy, sociable day. We had to get a move on to get to another meeting point to go on a Vespa Adventure.

What else was going to make us feel young again than a tour of the city on the back of a Vespa? I have always had a nostalgic appreciation of Vespas because my parents travelled from St Malo in the north of France to Cadaqués on the north-east coast of Spain in the 1950s, helmets slung over the handlebars. It's just not an image you would associate with either parent if you had met them years later. Personally, I have always had a love of two wheels ever since I had my own 50 cc trials motorbike when I was 16.

We got to the meeting point just in time and we took a seat outside a pub on a street corner. While we had our first beer, the heavens opened. Great, we thought. Not only are we going on motorbikes into some of the scariest traffic in the world (the city has nearly eight million registered motorbikes), but we are doing it after dark on wet roads. Just as well we planned to tell my mum after the event, not before. She still worries about me.

Ponchos were handed out. The second beer arrived in a plastic cup. We wondered why. It was because we were allowed to take it with us on the back of the Vespa. As if by magic, the rain stopped and off we went, in a convoy of half a dozen people who were up for the ride. It was exhilarating, great fun, the alcohol was never-ending, and the food fabulous, if too much of it. We ducked in and out of restaurants and bars with live music. And something else happened that is not within David's nature at all. He found himself singing along to and doing the actions for a live rendition of YMCA. It must have been all the free beer.

Backpacker street Bui Vien is better known for its night-time bars but on our last day in Ho Chi Minh City we found a breakfast café to write home about. At The Note we ordered a baguette and what turned out to be the best cappuccino of the entire trip. We headed up some steep wooden steps to the tiny seating area which had a view of the street below.

It was only then that we realised why the café was called The Note. You could write a note on a small square sticker and put it on the wall with all the others. The place was covered in them, from floor to ceiling, even in the loo and on the chairs.

I wrote one each for my children. For Seb, my first-born, I wrote in a heart: 'I hope one day you'll find this! Love you loads.'

Seb is on the autism spectrum. We are lucky that he is at the 'mild' end of the spectrum. I hesitate to use that term, because many people with Asperger Syndrome would not describe the ways in which their condition can affect them as mild. But you will know what I mean, he is at the lower end of the spectrum. And, for me, it certainly didn't seem mild when I was dealing with his behaviour at home and learning all about how best to parent him. Asperger Syndrome was not something I had ever heard of. At that time, all I knew about autism was what I had seen on the Tom Cruise and Dustin Hoffman film Rain Man.

Asperger Syndrome were the first two words I put into an internet search engine.

Seb's issues involved being over-sensitive to sounds, he loathed balloons in case they popped, his anger went from zero to off-the-scale in seconds. He found it difficult to be gracious when things didn't go his way playing football. He was happiest lining up his planes or playing with Lego.

The saddest thing was watching him walk into the school playground, to stand on the same drain cover each morning, waiting for the bell to ring (he hated the sound of it) while all around him children were running, playing, screaming, laughing.

I had started noticing his behaviours when he was three. He enjoyed spinning the wheels on his upside-down yellow truck and he was chased around the hairdressers when it came to having a haircut. He was the only child I knew who did this.

Seb was a picky eater. I decided early to pick my battles and I happily gave him a plate of instant noodles for Christmas lunch. Another year he had pizza. While the fight for a diagnosis continued, I tried him on a gluten-free and dairy-free diet and this, along with stripping out fizzy sugar-laden drinks, removed a lot of his anger. We tried brain-gym kind of exercises to improve his co-ordination, and we tried sound therapy, which he found calming.

In the struggle to get a diagnosis, I kept a diary of incidents and behaviours that I didn't consider 'normal' (I am not sure you can even say that any more). It was a struggle because, fortunately or unfortunately, Seb was borderline in getting a statement of need, which meant he was in danger of slipping through the net. In that diary, in September 2003, I wrote: 'At bedtime, tears in his eyes, Seb explains that he is not looking forward to the new school term tomorrow. Everyone hates him, he says. He is teased a lot by kids in his class. They call him dumb, stupid. He feels like he doesn't belong in this family because he makes mistakes all the time. I say I made mistakes as a child. But you weren't hated by everyone, he says.' He was ten.

I had to fight for a diagnosis which, eventually, was Asperger Syndrome with an element of dyspraxia. For me, diagnosis was key, it was a positive thing which meant that he got the right support at the right time, he went to the right school for him, and he accessed a youth inclusion project where he made some wonderful friends, who are still friends today. Seb took the help offered. When it came to exams, he had extra time and a quiet room. He achieved his target grades.

It was only when I met other parents at a conference that I felt for the first time that someone understood. No longer was my father going to believe that Seb's behaviour was something that a good old-fashioned smack could sort out.

Today Seb is a tall handsome young man (perhaps I am biased) who works full-time, lives independently, has some lovely friends and is one of the most inclusive young men I know. I am glad that he seems to have caught my travel bug and he has been on holiday with mates to Florida and Mexico as well as several cities around Europe. And he completed a ten-week Raleigh International expedition to Costa Rica and Nicaragua, which helped him become more self-aware and mindful as well as raising his awareness of conservation and the need to look after the environment.

The most important word here is friends. Genuine friends, some of whom are on the spectrum, some who aren't, some who have other disabilities or challenges. One of my happiest moments was when he had some friends around for his 16th birthday, just some of the lads, and they sat around with pizza and played the card game UNO. I listened from the next room, delighting in the fact that they were all loving the game, laughing heartily, and being so relaxed in their own company, far away from the judgment and bullying of the classroom.

He has been lucky to have three wonderful Alexanders in his life. One is still his best friend. They gelled in Seb's first year of secondary school where they met in what would now be called an additional resource centre. To us, it was

Room 5, a safe place to unwind and be quiet. I have never been prouder than when I heard Seb's speech in tribute to his friend, spoken as best man at Alex's wedding reception.

The second was someone who Seb got on well with at Cub Scouts. At one overnight camp they were in the same tent when the most almighty thunderstorm broke out. It went on for hours. Certainly no one got any sleep that night. Alexander could be heard in the tent, talking him through it. He would say, look, that was the lightning, now we are going to count to the thunder. See, it's going away. Such a nicer response than laughing at someone and telling them they are silly.

The third Alexander was a year older than him. I observed them playing pool together. Instead of being a competitive player, Alexander was nothing but encouraging. If Seb missed the ball or his cue went skewiff. Alex just said: 'Never mind, Seb, here, have another go.' Just the memory of it makes me emotional. Such a simple act of kindness at a young age. He probably had no idea of the impact it had. As a parent I know that Seb, who now helps to coach the Jersey Learning Disabilities Football Team, of which he is a member, would do just that for others.

The strange thing is that, despite having been such a picky eater as a child, he now eats an amazing array of food including vegetables, nuts and grains. In his 20s he has chosen to be vegetarian and he is as realistically vegan as he can be, if I can put it like that. The food that he makes for himself is healthy and delicious. If only someone had told me not to worry when all he would eat was four-minute packet noodles.

He is fortunate that autism does not cripple his life, but my own experience gave me a small insight into what other parents go through. With that in mind, I became a trustee for an autism charity for a year or two. Years later, when it came to getting out of journalism, I worked as a fundraiser for that same charity and David supported adult clients. We learned even more about the broad spectrum of autism and the huge challenges faced by parents. More than anything, I appreciated that autism does not go away. It's there, day in, day out.

Now, in this latest chapter of our lives, I realised that not since I had to fight for Seb's diagnosis nearly 20 years ago had I felt so passionate about something and, most importantly, what I could personally do about it. Animal rights was just something that I was going to have to shout about.

Tears at the killing tree

'Man's inhumanity to man
Makes countless thousands mourn.
Man was made to Mourn.'

—*Robert Burns*

The inevitable had happened. I woke up dreaming that I had been sick. I hadn't, but several visits to the loo made it obvious that Imodium was required. The timing of these things is never great. We were up at 5.15 am to catch a 6.30 bus from Ho Chi Minh City to Phnom Penh. Thankfully we always factored in some extra time so that we didn't run late and this was used to good effect for my toilet visits, while David checked out. First he had to find an ATM. We had been assured that the reception desk would take a card for payment. But not, apparently, on a Monday morning.

We checked in at the bus agency where we were to be picked up. I ran to the loo.

Luckily the bus was actually a comfortable eight-seater van. Over the years we had collected a few sick bags from airlines, with just such a day in mind. I was equipped with (and used) three. What a lifesaver.

Despite feeling so lousy, I was frustrated that I couldn't talk to the chatty Vietnamese family travelling with us. When we booked our tickets, the only two seats available were as far apart as they could be, David in the front seat and me at the back on the opposite side.

When the other passengers realised that we were together, they asked David if he would like to sit next to me. 'God, no,' he replied.

When I feel ill, I go quiet, very quiet. I don't want to move and I don't want to speak. It took effort to get out of the bus each time we stopped but I knew I should use the facilities, to put it politely.

Fortunately the border crossing out of Vietnam and into Cambodia was quiet and straightforward. I emerged sheepishly from the van hoping that there would be no queues. There weren't. Like a child clutching a lunchbox on their first day at school, I took my sick bag with me, just in case. The only thing we had to do at the border was go through a security scanner. I didn't want to put the sick bag in a bin in case I needed it again. There was nothing for it but to put it down on the conveyor belt and let it be subjected to inspection. Luckily, no one minded that I was carrying liquids though I was sure that there was more than 100 ml in the bag. I picked it up the other side and walked away.

Two minutes into Cambodia and I was retching again. The poor girl next to me was probably never more glad that she was wearing her face mask. Twice she reached into her handbag and passed me the most beautiful smelling, cool wet-wipe. I could have cried.

I thought I must be the passenger from hell but they all smiled sympathetically every time we got on and off the bus, although when one of them bought a hot dog on a stick and ate it en route I could have screamed. I couldn't bring myself to think about food and I certainly didn't want to think about what had given me Delhi Belly on Day 43.

David, however, continued to report 'all well in poo land'. His strategy was to eat anything, drink several beers and never use hand sanitiser. 'Hand sanitiser is for wimps,' he would declare. 'How can you ever build up resistance to bacteria if you don't ingest it first?'

The only time I thought that he had contracted something dreadful was when I saw a clump of brown dots on his foot. I pointed them out. He rubbed at them, thinking it was probably dirt. They didn't budge. They didn't itch. Then we noticed that he had matching dots on the other foot. Our diagnosis? It was the sun-tanned pattern from wearing Crocs non-stop for six weeks.

If our journey so far had started us thinking about animal welfare, what with elephants, bears and dogs, Cambodia was going to focus our minds on man's inhumanity to man. Even now, nearly 40 years after the end of the murderous Pol Pot regime, the seasonal rains erode the soil to the extent that fragments of bone and clothing are brought to the surface. We laughed politely at one guide's talk of flying cows until we realised that even today these poor beasts occasionally stand on a mine.

Every year in Cambodia, there are still deaths and injuries caused by live munitions and landmines and, despite concerted efforts to rid the country of them, it is estimated that it could be another 100 years before the painstaking work will be considered complete. Cambodia has some 40,000 amputees, one of the highest rates in the world.

Tourists to Cambodia still need to exercise care when going off the beaten track. Anyone wanting to rent a motor-cycle and ride the back roads of Siem Reap or Battambang provinces is well advised to ask about mine safety first.

It is shocking to learn what went on at the Killing Fields but they are a must-do for any visitor to the country, as is the Tuol Sleng Genocide Prison in Phnom Penh, and yet we were told that in secondary schools there is no formal study of the Pol Pot regime in an apparent failure to acknowledge events of the past.

We bought the book First They Killed My Father by Luong Ung, a harrowing autobiographical account of the brutal regime. Trained as a child soldier in a work camp for orphans, Luong at one point describes the moment when she witnesses a crowd deciding what to do with a captured Khmer Rouge soldier. She watches 'without emotion' as an old woman who has lost her children and grandchildren takes her revenge by hitting the prisoner with a hammer before a younger woman stabs him in the stomach with a knife.

It is hard to believe that Luong was recounting events that she saw when she was nine.

I remember reading about the Khmer Rouge when I was in sixth-form but it's only now that I have a real grasp of what went on here – within my lifetime. Between 1975 and 1979, two million civilians were slaughtered. A quarter of their population. A visit to Tuol Sleng was very sobering indeed, the faces of hundreds of innocent people staring out from photographs, people who were brought to this former school for torture and questioning.

A very good audio guide described the brutality, including holding people upside down until they were unconscious and then dunking their heads in a vat of filthy water and human excrement. And to think this could happen to someone just for wearing glasses. Most of the people who died, either from being murdered or through starvation, were innocent people like you and me.

There are 20,000 mass grave sites dotted around Cambodia. The largest of the killing fields is at Choeung Ek on the outskirts of Phnom Penh. Today it is home to the Genocidal Centre which serves as a monument to all those who died as well as an educational tool to ensure history never repeats itself. The Memorial Stupa, constructed in 1988, contains more than 8,000 skulls. It is astonishing to learn that this is just one of 300 killing fields.

We felt emotionally exhausted by the time we reached the 'killing tree' where the Khmer Rouge smashed babies' heads against the tree trunk. I fear that some parents had to witness it.

In striking contrast, there is the magic and beauty of Angkor Wat and the other temples dotted around Siem Reap. All have something to offer, whether it is the 200 faces in the Buddhist shrine Bayon, or the peace and quiet and beautiful carvings of Banteay Srei, or – everyone's favourite – the ruins of Ta Prohm where trees have grown through and around the temples.

Siem Reap itself is a safe, friendly place, with a large, old market. There are a lot of charming cafés, many of which are social enterprises, are benefitting the community or have lots of books. What more could you want?

We had arranged for a guide to show us around the temples for a couple of days. Samang was interesting, a lovely, smiley man. He used to be a monk but he gave it up after five years because he missed wearing underwear. Isn't it funny that I remember that more easily than I remember facts about Angkor Wat, one of the largest religious monuments in the world? I loved imagining what it must have been like for French explorer Henri Mouhot to stumble upon the temples in the mid-19th century. Although the temples hadn't exactly been 'lost', his writings stirred up new interest and helped lead to their popularity today.

We wondered exactly what happened to the civilisations that designed and constructed buildings of such grandeur and complexity.

We clambered around the temples and climbed more steps than we cared to count. One day my Health app recorded more than 19,000 steps and in the Flights Climbed section, it clocked up 17 floors. We were keeping up with the young backpackers, that's for sure, even if we were probably more aware of the dangerous drops and perilous staircases with little more than a thin rope to hold on to, if you were lucky.

Not since Halong Bay had we been conscious of the impact of tourism on a place. We were surprised to see how much access that we and hundreds of others had to the temples. Even where areas were taped off, tourists were climbing to get the best selfie view. We were pleased to see several of the authorised guides asking people politely to respect the signs and stay on the designated walkways. Nevertheless, the temples' popularity is surely going to take its toll. Some 2.5 million foreign tourists visit each year, bringing in more than $100 million, contributing significantly to the economy but also contributing significantly to wear and tear. And here we were, adding to it. We wondered again how tourism will change in the future, when everyone is aware of their carbon footprint and how World Heritage Sites might need greater protection.

A lot of what we were seeing could be read about in guide books but it was the more recent personal history that fascinated us. Our guide explained how his own parents were brought together by an arranged marriage. Hundreds of other couples were ordered by the Khmer Rouge to marry and have more children. On the communal wedding day they were fed a feast and were expected to consummate the marriage that night, even though some couples had never even met before. Samang's father, having been in the army, knew that they must obey and he respectfully advised his new wife accordingly. The next day, all couples were asked if they had done the deed. They all said yes, but not all were telling the truth. Those who lied didn't realise that they had been spied upon all night – and were executed on the spot.

Time and time again, we were reminded how precarious life could be here in Cambodia, especially in the rural areas. Rainy season was upon us and it was a good time to head 16 km out of Siem Reap to see the floating village of Kompung Phluk, Harbour of the Tusks. All the buildings are on stilts, including houses, schools and the police station. The 3,000 villagers know to expect the rising waters of Tonle Sap Lake. When we visited, boats were being prepared for the higher water levels which were imminent.

We took a shallow boat out to the mangroves. Suddenly we realised how much we were sitting ducks for people selling their wares. We passed a string of boats which were selling Pringles and Fanta as well as writing books and pencils for the kids. We pulled up next to one, clearly the friend or sister of our boat woman. Thinking I was being kind, I bought a couple of soft drinks, but then the hard sell started. The seller started by asking if I'd like to buy something for the plump captain. I offered her a drink. She reached forward and grabbed the biggest bag of biscuits. Then the retailer started on about her three children, one of them lying half-naked next to her, fast asleep.

I agreed to take some text books and pencils. Before I knew it I had been fleeced of $25. I clearly hadn't been thinking straight. The woman then paddled furiously back to the homes so that we could give them out. It was partly worth it for the look on some of the kids' faces – some (by no means all) were absolutely delighted and grateful.

It was a fascinating, if frustrating, day out, even if we had felt we had been taken for a ride. It had also felt a bit like a human zoo, walking down a street taking photos of people's real lives.

Naked children were splashing around in the water. I wouldn't fancy it myself, it was brown with mud, and there was too much rubbish, something that would surely only increase as the lake swelled in the coming weeks. It wouldn't take much for some of those wooden stilts to collapse or for a storm to bring many of them down like a pack of cards. Our minds were drawn to Kerala which had seen its worst flooding for a century. We started to monitor developments with interest, as we were due to be there in a month. We needed to play for time, so we booked a flight out of Siem Reap, via Bangkok, to Colombo.

The scars on Sri Lanka

'People started to run'
—*Quote in tsunami museum in Perilaya*

Sometimes, getting deals with your hotel booking is just not worth it. I chose a hotel because it came with a free transfer from Colombo's Bandaranaike International Airport. So that we didn't have to rush, we decided to stay overnight at a hotel near the airport before heading south to Hikkaduwa. I really wish we had not. Between the airport and the hotel, the driver casually asked if we had forward plans. Beyond four nights in Hikkaduwa, we did not. We said that we would be happy to hear some suggestions, which we were expecting by email.

The next morning, instead of taking us straight down the coast, the driver took us a few streets away, down a dusty lane and he parked outside an unmarked building. It turned out to be a hotel. Large black gates closed behind us. I had the creeps from the start. I tried not to worry. David was as unconcerned as had he walked into a branch of Thomas Cook on the high street.

I observed that it was quite a new hotel but there were no signs of guests. We were offered tea and coffee, which irked me no end because I was keen to get going. Before we knew it, they had produced a map and we discussed the places that we hoped to visit. The hotel owner was obviously the boss. He was a short man dressed in a black shirt and black trousers and I just couldn't warm to him, not even when he took me on a little tour of his hotel grounds while the other staff members rallied around and did some research and some maths. They came up with a figure for ten days which included accommodation and a driver. By this time, I couldn't think straight, I couldn't work out the dollar-rupee exchange rate and when put on the spot I couldn't work out how much I would normally have been paying per night. Maybe they had put something in the tea, I thought.

David hates negotiating. He would have accepted the first price and thought they were doing us a favour. I was flummoxed and just a tad intimidated. I wondered what would happen if we declined and asked to leave. Instead, I got them to give us a bit of a discount but not because I had done any clever calculations. By now, I thought, I should be a savvy traveller and yet here I was feeling anything but.

I was even more worried when the boss hopped in the car with us. I thought maybe we would drop him somewhere along the way, but he stayed all the way to Hikkaduwa, all 100 km of it. At one point, out of the blue, he asked about our religion. To me, nothing felt 'right' and I spent the next few days becoming completely paranoid. I was convinced that either a) the driver would not turn up to honour our schedule exploring Sri Lanka or b) we would be collected by the boss and kidnapped. This had not been helped by the fact that I had recently read about issues in the country, something about terrorists plotting in tourist bars. I can't fully remember the details and have not been able to find the reference since, but the events of Easter Sunday 2019 have perhaps vindicated some of my thinking.

As it happened, Kumar, our driver, turned up on the dot at 8 am and, I was relieved to see, alone.

In reality, what was far more concerning was that Kumar had already driven for three hours and was in danger of falling asleep at the wheel. I spent the journey scrutinising him in the mirror, opening windows to let in a blast of air and making inane conversation. At one point, I prodded him sharply in the back and asked if he was wide awake.

My thoughts were dominated by one thing once we were on the south-west coast of Sri Lanka. Hikkaduwa was devastated by the Boxing Day tsunami of 2004. As I stared out to the Indian Ocean, I imagined what it must have been like. It was now the end of August and the sea was quite rough. The breakers smashed onto the shore and there was a heavy drag backwards. There were always some swimmers out, including children, but despite being a reasonably good swimmer myself I decided it was too strong to be a comfortable dip. The sea easily tossed people about and pushed them over.

What would the tsunami have sounded like? Didn't people think it was unusual that the tide had gone out a kilometre? What would I have done in the aftermath? Escaped to an airport as soon as possible or stayed to help with the clear-up? Children who lost parents, parents who lost children, homes and businesses washed away in seconds. The sights and smells of dead bodies, bloated by the water and swollen with the heat. We saw homes which have not been rebuilt since the tsunami. Maybe a whole family perished or, in some cases, families have moved inland, too scared to rebuild their lives in the same place, so close to the sea.

An informal tsunami museum at Perilaya is run by a lady called Kamani, in a building that was (and is) her home. She has collected many photos and witnesses' stories to explain the devastation of the day. Nearby, a giant Buddha looks out to sea, holding the pose for fearlessness and protection. We had read that its height represents the maximum height of the wave though it seemed impossible and it didn't say that on the official plaques. Over the road, right at the edge of the beach, a memorial depicts the world's worst train disaster. More than 1,700 passengers on the Queen of the Sea were killed after the surge of water lifted the train carriages off the tracks and tossed them around like toys. Hundreds of people are buried here.

We went to Seenigama where a friend and former newspaper colleague volunteered for a couple of months in 2005. She later brought their volleyball team over to Jersey for a beach tournament. We decided to walk the 2 km or so from Hikkaduwa, even though it would have been easier to take a tuk-tuk. You notice so much more on foot, not least the number of derelict properties and the small houses with a gravestone or two in their garden. To cut a long story short, we found Adesh, a man who knew my friend. Even though we had turned up without notice, he greeted us warmly. Having cut open some fresh coconuts for us, he showed us photos of his Jersey visit with the volleyball team and he asked after other people he met in the Island.

The charitable foundation that he works with continues to run free medical and dental clinics, as well as psychological counselling. And the volleyball team still plays. It had been really important for the children to have had a focus with the sport. As Adesh said, how do you measure the psychological benefit of having fun on a beach after such a devastating tragedy?

Hello, how are you? Where are you from? It always starts the same. The opening gambit of someone wanting to talk to you. In Sri Lanka they have the patter down to a fine art. But you know what's coming. Tuk-tuk, sir? I have a tuk-tuk, I can take you to the lagoon, the turtle hatchery, the tea factory, the temple, whatever.

It seemed that everyone had a tuk-tuk or something to sell, even the waiters in a beachside restaurant. You think they are being friendly and the next thing you know they are showing you their driving licence and offering to take you somewhere for 400 rupees. 'Good price.'

And even when you get a tuk-tuk to take you somewhere, they often make a detour to a herbal ayurvedic garden, wood-carving shop or gem museum. And there the hard sell starts. They immediately say they will give a good price and they readily halve the marked price (if indeed you are lucky to find such a thing). You think you must be getting a bargain but you struggle to keep up with working out an exchange rate. By the time you have converted it to pounds, you are on the tuk-tuk home again with a bag of stuff you didn't mean to buy. And then you wonder what commission the tuk-tuk driver must be on.

The man who showed us around his pretty average herbal garden even had the cheek to suggest we tip him for the time he spent showing us around (about ten minutes). We didn't. And he asked for David's red cara-biner for his son. I muttered something like: 'It'll cost you 200 rupees.'

It often felt like everything in Sri Lanka amounted to hard sell. If you agreed to buy one item, they pushed you to buy a second. If you bought a soft drink, they pushed you to buy a snack. If you opted for the small portion, they pushed you to buy the larger size. It was starting to annoy me.

We took a tuk-tuk to Unawatuna. On the way, our trusty driver decided he knew best and took us via Galle. Fair enough, we went along with it. We remember it now as the place where we walked around the grounds of a fort, where we had the misfortune to see a man with a monkey on the end of a piece of string, and another man carrying a cobra in a sack.

Are these things illegal? We think they may be. We were not particularly surprised to see it, but we were astonished to see western tourists paying a few rupees to take a photo or interact with the animal in some pointless way.

In Unawatuna, instead of being taken to a main street or beach, we got dropped off in the grounds of a hotel which, it turned out, belonged to the driver's 'friend'. Of course it did. And no doubt he got a healthy little backhander, thank you. I wouldn't have minded if it had happened occasionally but it seemed to be ingrained in their DNA and I was starting to tire of it. Sometimes I felt like I was shunning people who might have genuinely wanted to say hello or children who just wanted to practise their English. One day, taking a brief walk around a tea plantation in the hills, I really wasn't in the mood. A persistent little boy carrying a large empty plastic bottle lurked around us. 'Photo,' he said. 'Photo.'

So in the end David took his photo and then the boy said: 'Money.' We opted to give him a 20-rupee note. It really wasn't much, 10p or something, but maybe it would mean a little more to him. However, a little further on, there were four more kids. Two started walking our way saying:

'Photo.' An old woman further up, standing outside her home — even she said: 'Photo.' At which point I walked in the opposite direction with tears in my eyes.

It's difficult, really. I know that they don't want foreigners just turning up and snapping away at their home life. I appreciate that they must see us with our cameras and guess that we must have spent hundreds if not thousands of pounds to have travelled all this way. It wasn't the money that mattered so much as the principle. If in six months we gave money, however small, to every person we would like to photograph, our budget would be worn away pretty fast. What is an authentic experience in the world these days anyway?

Everybody who visits Mirissa will know that it is considered to be one of Sri Lanka's finest spots for whale watching. Now, I am not particularly mad keen on seeing whales in the wild. I am all for watching Sir David Attenborough do his Blue Planet thing so that I can enjoy it from the best seat in the house with a mug of hot chocolate.

But it seemed to be the only thing to do. A boat was booked and off we went. We were on the top deck where the seats were squashed in together and everyone seemed to be hemmed in by barriers. It was very odd. I was glad that at least we were given lifejackets.

We set off in glorious sunshine. We were given snacks and bottles of water for breakfast. I was quite distracted by watching the staff to see if they were going to retrieve all of the rubbish and make sure it didn't fall in the water. How much better would it have been had they not distributed plastic bottles in the first place?

We motored out for a good hour. It was when David realised we could no longer see land that he felt a bit, well, scared. Not that he let on. We both went quiet, him because of fear, me because I felt queasy. And then there was a spout. Not a whale, just a spout. And we were off, going as fast as we could. People leapt to their feet, climbing out from behind their barriers, full of whoops of joy and ridiculous excitement. They all headed to one side of the boat. They were squealing. I didn't get it. I wanted to see the whales but not at any cost to my safety and preferably peacefully, with no disruption to the whale itself.

Dark clouds were approaching and we could see where it was hammering down with rain up ahead. Surely the captain would steer clear of it and stay in the calm over here?

No, that was where the whale was and that's where we were going. In through a curtain of rain which one minute was vertical and then became horizontal, scattering everyone downstairs. Those who had had the best view up front were drenched within seconds and they beat a hasty retreat. Thanks to the railings around our seats, I didn't feel I could move easily, and feeling queasy makes me want to not move at all so that is what I did. Rigid and silent and wet.

David admitted later that this was the only time in our entire journey that he felt our lives had been at risk. You hear so many stories of unscrupulous, untrained, inexperienced and unregulated chancers operating all sorts of seagoing adventures and, as much as you try to check credentials, you really have to put your trust in many people.

David stayed rigid and silent and petrified. At one point we exchanged glances, pretending we were having fun.

Another spout, the back of a whale, a tail. Super-excitement again. We had seen a whale and its baby. We were told that the red stuff in the water was their poo, red because of the amount of krill they eat. Great over-empha-sised laughter and whooping. I couldn't stand it.

Once we had seen a whale or two, the skipper clearly felt he had fulfilled his brief and announced we were heading back to land, a good hour less than advertised. We were not complaining. We couldn't get back soon enough.

I regretted going on the whale-watching boat but not as much as I regret contributing to the misery of the killer whales in SeaWorld in Florida by attending their show as recently as 2008. But it's a great illustration of how change can and does happen. Just look at the public outcry after the release of the 2013 documentary Blackfish, which told the story of one of SeaWorld's performing killer whales, Tilikum, which killed several people while in captivity. Interviews with former trainers and camera footage revealed what goes on behind the scenes, not least the capture of the whales and the dreadfully cruel and confined spaces they are kept in.

SeaWorld's response to Blackfish was to announce that they would stop breeding them and they would phase out orca performances.

When we had visited, we enjoyed watching shows fea-turing dolphins that had been trained to jump through hoops and whales that could toss a wetsuited trainer into the air. We swam with dolphins at Discovery Bay. We never ques-tioned it. How was Tilikum captured? How did Shamu, the original orca from the 1960s, die? How many 'Shamus' have there been? How many trainers have been killed due to the frustration and anger of the whales? What effect did cap-tivity, transport and separation from their pods have on these beautiful creatures? What is the state of their mental health?

We would not go anywhere near these shows now. And doesn't that just demonstrate how we can change our thinking? If we can change our thinking on dolphins, plastic, smoking and gender, why can't we when it comes to eating animals?

Overall, we loved our time in Sri Lanka, not least for the photography, and the fact that we survived without being kidnapped. In ten days we packed in the heritage of Anuradhapura, the stunning rock temples of Dambulla, the climb up Lion Rock at Sigiriya, the train to Ella. What I will remember most is paddling with a wild turtle at Hikkaduwa and the beauty of the Royal Botanical Gardens near Kandy, where we spent our ninth wedding anniversary. The impressive gardens, bigger than we expected, were full of fabulous trees, beautifully kept parkland and exotic flowers, with a stop for Ceylon tea and a banana split to boot.

Going out on to the balcony of our hotel room felt exciting because everything reminded us how close we were to India — the heat, the smell, the sounds and the sights. From our large comfortable bed, we could see the sun coming up over the mountains. A great buffet breakfast was served on the top floor, where we could appreciate the sun bouncing off the huge Buddha face on the hillside.

David loved the fact that Sri Lanka is one of the most richly biodiverse places on earth. Hardly a day went by without chancing upon a number of magnificent monitor lizards. A slow amble around the lake in Kandy had us excitedly photographing cormorants, egrets and their chicks, bats, pelicans, terrapins and turtles. Less exciting were the few dead fish on the lakeside, the occasional blackbird pecking out an eye. And it was distressing to see, next to the Temple of the Tooth, a huge open truck carrying an elephant, chained and roped in place. It was obvious that there had been a festival — street dogs had red bindis on their foreheads. We had no idea where the elephant lived or how far he had to travel. So sad for such a magnificent beast. He had the best full tusks I have ever seen.

We took a jeep safari in Yala National Park, where we saw black and white kingfishers, ibis, eagles, parakeets, kites, toucans, vervot monkeys, deer with beautiful antlers and water buffalo. In the last 15 minutes we drove out of the park and onto the main road where we saw a wild elephant. People were throwing fruit to him. I wondered how wild he really was. I'd be pretty wild if I was disturbed by jeep-loads of tourists confronting me, even if they were armed with bananas.

There are about 7,500 wild elephants in Sri Lanka but there is a problem keeping them away from villages, where they can cause serious damage and destruction — a real hazard to life and crops. We read a report online (www.news24.com) that said elephants had killed 375 people in the last five years, but villagers retaliated by slaughtering 1,200 of them. That's hardly fair, is it? I can understand the need to protect humans but there is a greater need to protect the elephants. And we are supposed to be the intelligent ones, so it really should be possible to find a healthy balance.

The beaches on the south coast were stunning but the sea, with its boisterous breakers, was startlingly strong. It didn't make for a relaxing swim and we certainly couldn't go snorkelling. But I realised (I knew it anyway) that our beaches back home in Jersey are the best you'll find anywhere in the world. I just wish our sea was a little warmer, but our coast-line is as unspoilt as you will find anywhere.

In Sri Lanka, much as the beaches looked pretty from a distance but when we got close we noticed the rubbish at the edges and, for a resort of such beauty, it was not good enough. We love the chaos of a place, the character, the smells, but we never want to see litter on a beach.

Food was cheap and 'safe'. So many places catered for the tourist that we were never far from pizza, pasta and chips if that is what we needed, rather than roti, curry and rice.

Sri Lanka, the Pearl of Asia, is beautiful, in an Asian kind of way. Miles of unspoilt countryside, palm trees, forests, national parks, tea plantations. But then, heading into towns, sprawling shanty rundown huts, many now unoccupied and much new building.

On the drive in to Kandy, we noticed that small shops, crammed with goods, seemed to have limited power supply. The lightbulbs were weak. These were interspersed with the occasional modern 'supercentre', upmarket gem store or small blue church. Rusty coloured short-haired dogs slept in the gutters, right behind the wheels of parked cars.

Particularly smart walled-off office buildings seemed to be reserved for those who are considered important, like the Central Provincial Irrigation Department or the Office of the Registrar of Pesticides. The dusty buses looked like they had been on the road for 100 years. The school holiday traffic in Kandy was busier than anywhere we had seen in Sri Lanka. Everyone fought for position on the road, drivers would try to overtake even when there was neither the reason nor the space to do so.

Toy monkeys with long thin arms hugging the back of tuk-tuks amused me, as did messages like 'You'r (sic) follow me but you don't back kiss me'. Mis-spelt signs also made me smile. A shop selling 'Shoes and Sleepers'. And it seemed that every shop or service was the 'best' or included a 'lucky', a 'palace' or a 'majestic', reminding us of The Best Exotic Marigold Hotel, the inspiration for the next step of our journey.

Turns out I'm a bit of an eco-warrior

'Be kind to all creatures. This is the true religion'
—*Buddha*

Much to my amusement, David can well up when opening a new jar of Indian Spiced Apple Chutney. Such is his love for India. He admits that he has, before now, also had a lump in his throat when opening our spice cupboard, catching sight and smell of our garam masala, cumin and turmeric purchased in Khari Baoli, Old Delhi, Asia's largest wholesale spice market.

I have never really been an inspirational cook. I get by and I can do a roast and I have managed to feed a family, but I don't think I do much that is truly special. I take after my mum. No disrespect intended. We had typical 1970s food, she would make a big bolognese sauce which we considered exotic (Italian!) which we would have two days running, she would make a big stew with dumplings which would also last two days, we would have faggots cooked in their own modern foil tray, we would have fish fingers with deep-fried chips, and sausage and mash. In my notebooks I have recipes for her trifle and her bacon and egg pie (we weren't posh enough to call it quiche). It's a family joke that when she first tried making prawn cocktail for her birthday, she made us all ill and we never had it at home again.

My childhood was happy. I enjoyed my own company and would play in my bedroom contentedly for hours. I liked nothing better than being on the beach, looking for shells. I can still tell you the names of not only limpets and periwinkles but also Gibbula magus and Venerupis corrugata. I certainly know my thin tellins from my dog cockles. Looking for shells on the sand gives me a sense of peace. I don't know, maybe it does something to the brain like knitting or doing jigsaws. (Now, looking at everything with new eyes, I wonder whether people will criticise me for collecting shells. Of course, I don't condone exotic shell collecting by people who get rid of the shellfish just to sell the shell, but a few redundant bivalves picked up off a beach shouldn't matter, should they?)

The other thing that I enjoyed from an early age was spelling. My dad, who set up a home printing press in retirement, mostly cluttering up the dining-room table, used to hold spelling bees at tea time. I clearly recall being annoyed that my sister could spell 'phlegm' when I couldn't. Once learned, never forgotten. I had an inner competitiveness I didn't know I had.

Both my parents enjoyed word play and puns and we grew up with Scrabble and crosswords. It appeals to me now that 'veganism' is an anagram of 'saving me'.

As a child, I enjoyed Willard Price adventures which told the stories of Hal and Roger Hunt who helped capture animals for their father. He was described in the books as an animal collector. The animals would be sold to zoos, circuses and nature parks. They were, as so many things can be, of their time.

But how slow does change have to be? Poaching is still a big problem. While we were in Sri Lanka, it seemed that my Facebook feed kept highlighting trophy hunters, rich bastards who pay money to shoot wildlife. Doesn't this belong to a bygone age? Before we knew any better? It distresses me to think about magnificent wild animals being shot just because someone wants a photo next to their dead body or their head stuffed and hung on their wall. How is it still happening? Why, particularly when you can get just as big a thrill or adrenaline rush from computer games? Go kill virtual ones, for God's sake.

Soon, it might be the only ones we've got left.

It's only once you realise that you might have some autism in the family that you look back for clues in yourself. I was the kind of child who would not flinch when I had an injection. While other young girls were whimpering, I just took it in the arm, not believing it to be any big deal, and I didn't like the fuss that others made. I grew into a teenager who liked to be a bit different, although I suppose you could argue that all teenagers are like that. If everyone fancied Starsky, I preferred Hutch. While friends got school colours for tennis and hockey, I preferred trampolining. Everyone was rooting for Bjorn Borg while I seemed to be the only person cheering on John McEnroe. I liked having my own mind and I was perfectly happy in my own company.

To this day, I feel more like an observer in life than a participant, something I notice even more keenly in large crowds of people.

If someone had mentioned vegetarianism to me in my early teens, I probably would have embraced it because it was different. I wish I had heard a speaker like vegan activist Earthling Ed when I was a teenager. I'm a big fan of Ed Winters, who tells us that eating animals has no place in contemporary society. You allow animals to be killed for one meal that you forget instantly and you cost them their entire existence. What right as a species, he asks, do we have to do that?

Schools and colleges are just some of the places where he spreads the word. Ask yourself why you eat animals, he says. Maybe it is habit, most likely it is because it's what your parents taught you. As he eloquently points out, culture and tradition are not good benchmarks for morality. How do you morally justify taking the life of an animal just because we always have done?

Having left school with three admittedly mediocre A-levels, I took my parents by surprise when I came down from my bedroom one day to announce that I was going travelling from London to Kathmandu. With tickets already booked, they wouldn't be able to talk me out of it.

The article I wrote for my local paper afterwards was published under the headline 'Hostility and pure happiness on the road to Kathmandu' and described the happiest three months of my life. I set off totally unprepared but you don't realise how naive you are until you have that wonderful gift called hindsight. I had a small flimsy frame backpack, my father's ancient tweed 'grip', no Imodium and not enough cash.

My diary of the time reflects the everyday concerns of food, finances and bowel movements. But it also reminds me of many experiences, some fabulous, some frightening.

I went skinny-dipping in the Dead Sea on my 19th birthday, I heard gunfire on the streets of Damascus (it's ok, I was told, it's just the soldiers aiming at dogs for target practice), I sat cross-legged on the floor of some stranger's house to have dinner in Palmyra, I got groped in a shop in Jerusalem, I rode on horseback down the canyon to see the Treasury at Petra, I argued about women's rights with a teacher in an Iranian café (really not advisable), I was horrified by explicit photographs of beheaded Iraqi soldiers, being sold in Isfahan as postcards, I rode on the roof of a minibus as the driver navigated by the stars through the Baluchistan Desert, I was proposed to by a Pakistani stranger before my train left the station, I fended off a potential attacker in the shower in a Lahore campsite, I saw bears on chains in the slums of Delhi, I was moved by the Hindu ceremony on the river Ganges at Varanasi, and by the dead cow which floated past our boat, I was sick outside my tent in the Himalayas while being stared at by small Nepalese children, I had bartered like my life depended on it.

By the end, I kept telling shopkeepers and rickshaw drivers that I had no money, because I really didn't. I was scrimping and saving and borrowing off fellow travellers. I came back scrawny (Mum was horrified), I had suffered heat and sun stroke, lost about six kilos and one pink ankle sock. But I had gained 20 mosquito bites on the sole of one foot, a taste for travel and a particular love for India, though perhaps not enough to make me cry at the smell of aloo gobi mix.

I sat in a church once, seeking answers, praying for something to be meaningful. I can't remember why I was there, but it was not far from the primary school which my children attended. Maybe I had ten minutes before school pickup, which seems a ridiculous guess as I never felt like I had ten minutes to spare. I had the church to myself and I sat there, looking around, wondering what it was all about. I was going through a divorce and I wanted some higher being to guide me. I walked out feeling a little let down. I just didn't 'get' religion. It wasn't there on that day and it has evaded me ever since.

Although I am not religious, I can of course appreciate a good temple or a stunning cathedral as much as anyone. Choral music is some of the most beautiful ever written and I enjoy pieces like the sublime Requiem by Mozart, hymns and Christmas carols, the likes of which I had to learn by heart in primary school and in a parish church choir. I loved dressing up in a black cassock and white surplice when I was about nine or ten, for choir practice on a Wednesday and the service on Sunday. Weddings and funerals were equally exciting for they brought with them the reward of a can of Coke and a packet of crisps.

A few years ago David and I visited St Peter's Basilica in Vatican City. I watched as young tourists stood in the shafts of the sun's rays, a natural spotlight just made to satisfy today's appetite for selfies. They looked about as religious as I felt. What struck me more than anything was how much wealth is in the church and how it might be better redistributed in the world. I had given up looking for God a long time ago.

India is such a melting pot of different religions, Hindus, Muslims, Buddhists, Sikhs, Jains. And Christians, of course. My father would be proud that I don't really believe in anything. He blamed religion for all that was bad in the world. I do find it difficult to work out which I would choose if I were pushed for an answer. Buddhist, I suppose, on the grounds that they are kind to all creatures and they are peaceful people.

As we moved through India, occasionally feeling like we were 'a bit templed out', it was nonetheless fascinating to learn more about Hinduism. Hindus really do seem to worship everything but they don't have to go to the temple to do so. Everything can be a manifestation of their god but they are pretty pragmatic and flexible.

In Delhi our attention was drawn to colourful tiles on the external walls of a temple, tiles which depicted many different gods from different religions. There was a good reason. It meant that no one would take a pee against their walls. Except dogs and atheists perhaps.

We tried to work out what our own values were. What drives our decisions and actions, what influences what we do and who we are? Sometimes it's difficult to pinpoint what is important or even why but, for me, everything seemed to come back to one word and that was compassion. If you had asked me ten years ago, I am not sure that compassion was even on my radar but I very much hope it is now with me for the rest of my life.

Ahimsa. Gandhi believed in Ahimsa. An important tenet of Hinduism, Buddhism and Jainism, it decrees that all living beings have the spark of divine spiritual energy. It says that violence towards all living beings has karmic consequences. Ahimsa was the highest virtue as far back as 500 BC. Somehow, I feel, it has been forgotten along the way.

David was born on Boxing Day, two days after his father died. He doesn't analyse it too much.

A brush with cancer in his 40s brought a new perspective on life, as he considered the possibility that his number was up much sooner than he had hoped. It took just three months from the time he noticed that his left testicle was way more solid than it should be to the time he had it replaced with a silicone one, just in time for our honeymoon.

In his 25 years as a paramedic he saw things he would have preferred not to and, as with many who work in the emergency services, developed a capacity to file things away in the brain that need not be re-examined. The most harrowing experience was when he had the misfortune to be first on scene at the Victoria Crescent murders in 2011, when Damian Rzeszowski killed his wife, two young children, his father-in-law, a family friend and her five-year-old daughter, something that is a particularly rare occurrence in a quiet place like Jersey.

David likes nothing better than throwing himself into a debate on Facebook especially when it comes to ethical judgments, or where it might wind up others. He's the kind of person who will deliberately leave a £5 note in a pocket of a jacket he's giving to a charity shop.

Once, he took a patient back to a psychiatric care facility. While they were chatting, the man happened to mention that he loved Reader's Digest but being on minimal pocket money, he couldn't afford to pay for them. When he got home, David set up and paid for a subscription for him. It was a shame that the man didn't live long enough to see the first edition arrive in the post.

In semi-retirement David discovered a love of photography. We had many a discussion about whether five cameras was too much to pack for a six-month break. He won the day.

A full six months before we left, he got his suitcase out and I kept nagging him about its weight. With about three months to go, he revealed that he had removed the brick and so it would now be lighter and I had no need to worry. To this day, I am not sure whether he put a brick in it or not, but I decided to stop worrying. After all, it would be him carrying the damn thing and him paying for any excess baggage which, remarkably, we never did.

David's first wife, Della, the mother of my stepsons, was disabled. She had spina bifida and hydrocephalus. When she was born, she was put on a slab to see if she would survive the hour. Indomitable from the start, she certainly did survive. For most of her life, she was wheelchair-bound but she wasn't going to let it stop her. Most likely in her adult life, she would have lived in a home had she not met David, who was a volunteer minibus driver. They married. She got pregnant but they lost their first child, Amanda, who arrived way too early due to the sort of kidney infection that complicates the lives of many with paraplegia. She was advised not to have another pregnancy because the recurrent infections had left her with poor kidney function but she went on to have James, born a little prematurely days before Christmas and in a critical condition over the festive period. She was advised not to have another. She went on to have Ben.

Today both are fine, healthy young men of whom she would be enormously proud. Despite her early prognosis, she lived to the age of 48, having seen her youngest son turn 18. Ironically, she had received a long-awaited kidney transplant which had gone very well but subsequently succumbed to a chest infection as a result of the immuno-suppressant drugs she needed for her body to accept the kidney.

Della was the first disabled person that I really knew. And by coincidence she is immortalised in a report and photo in my first cuttings book. I had been writing for my local newspaper since I was 14 and had interviewed her on board the Lord Nelson, a fully accessible sailing boat. She answered my questions and I thought she had enjoyed herself. David tells me she hated it.

Despite her poor prognosis, Della married, had children (her fondest ambition), owned a house and travelled to London, Paris, the Pyrenees and Disney World in Florida. Despite many challenges and setbacks, she would reflect near the end of her life that she had achieved much more than she had ever hoped for.

As I neared my 50th birthday, a group of my old school friends embarked upon an A to Z challenge — 26 challenges to complete in the lead-up to our big birthdays. They ranged from coasteering to pole dancing, from clay pigeon shooting to holding a tarantula. Much of the fun was to be had in making letters fit. At one point, a suggestion for V was 'Volleyball in fat suits'. Instead we went aerial trekking and it became V for Vertigo. Actually, it proved to be too much of a challenge for one of our number and will forever be known as V for Vomit. What would Q, X and Z be? (Q for Quiver, an archery lesson; X for a charitable annual Xmas soup kitchen; and Z was for Zumba, quite original at the time, though I really wanted to go careering down a hill inside a Zorb ball.) There was much debate and a lot of giggles to be had over a bottle or two of wine.

U was quite easy to choose and to organise. U was for Udder. As Jersey girls, we decided we needed to try milking a cow by hand. We introduced ourselves to a dairy farmer and he said yes, of course. So, on with the wellies on a cold damp day, we headed to a dairy farm to see behind the scenes. I have no doubt that the farmer loves his cows and that this is as near to best practice as you could ask for in the dairy industry. We squirmed as we pulled a teat to make it spurt a white liquid, sufficient to create a lot more laughter. Not one to be squeamish, I was surprised that I really didn't like it, but we all drank the milk fresh from the cow and I certainly didn't see any reason to go vegan.

Actually, it was the same group of friends that gave me my first test in being vegetarian. Because we have known each other for so long, they were surprised and a little sceptical about my decision. We were all going round to one person's house for dinner (V for Vomit girl actually) and I asked ahead what she would be cooking. It had something to do with chicken. I said it was fine, I would have what they were having, I could just pick the chicken out of it. I didn't want to make a fuss. But I came away feeling that I had capitulated too soon and that I was really going to have to stand up for myself and stop trying to please everyone. This was the first lesson.

The process continued to be gradual. While we were travelling, David was the one who was happy to continue eating some seafood. After having a prawn pad thai, however, we decided to research why prawns should be off the menu. Eyestalk ablation is what did it. Most females in prawn farms have their eyes sliced open or cut off. Destroying the eyestalk gland encourages spawning. To coin a modern phrase, what the actual fuck?

Who even discovers this is possible? Who carries it out? Who allows it to continue? How cruel can we be? Where do we stop?

Another weird thing is isinglass, a form of collagen obtained from the dried swim bladders of fish and used in the processing of some beers and wines. I mean, who even discovered what could be done with such a thing in the first place? I feel sure that there must be some manmade alternative by now so that we can leave those poor damned fish to swim in the sea.

'How about we still eat things that don't have a face?' David ventured. He was thinking scallops, mussels, that kind of thing. Are shellfish any less sentient than animals, birds and fish? But they play an important part of the eco-system, I argued, we don't want to kill turtles in the process, we don't want their industries adding to the rubbish that pollutes the oceans. Scallops have eyes and will swim away from danger.

The more we read about pretty much everything we had been eating on a regular basis, the more we were horrified. Over many plant-based meals on our journey, we reflected on how we got to this point, of all the things that we had done in our lives, not knowing any better.

I got my first summer job at the age of 12 delivering full-fat Jersey milk in Tetrapaks. It was 1976, the year of a very hot summer and a drought. It was fun perching on the back of an open milk truck, constantly being reminded by the milkman to put the cartons in the shade. I would earn 50p for each milk round and, if I was lucky, a lukewarm yogurt. Very fancy.

At 14 I had my first work experience at the local newspaper and my very first job was to write a short report (ahem, on a manual typewriter) on the opening of the disabled toilets at Jersey Zoo.

Coincidentally, around this time, David would have been volunteering at the Zoo. He had a love of snakes and tortoises and he helped out at the new Gaherty Reptile Breeding Centre. He recalls being allowed to help himself to chicks reared as food for some of the predators in captivity. They were a much-appreciated snack for his polecats at home. The chicks had to be killed and the methodology in those days was to throw them to the ground as forcefully as possible which, he says, seemed to kill them instantly. He didn't think twice about it. It was just what was done.

On occasion, he would dispatch mice in a similar fashion, so they could be fed to reptiles.

Only during our journey did he drop into the conversation something that had just never come up before ('Honey, I'm a murderer') that he had shot calves with a bolt gun for feeding to the Asiatic lions and bears. Again, at the time and since, he had never thought much of it, it certainly didn't keep him awake at night, but he did hope that death was swift and he is comfortable with the fact that he knew he dealt with the calf as humanely as he could.

As we reflected on previous holiday employment, he had one more confession to make. He loved helping out on a friend's large dairy farm, mostly gathering the hay crop, but he remembers on one occasion assisting when the calves were disbudded. Disbudding and de-horning are common practice in the dairy industry, considered necessary to prevent injuries to farm workers as well as other animals, but they are surely painful when done without anaesthetic or due veterinary care. As far as I am aware, it is not just like cutting your toenails.

If we think these things are horrible, we just have to remind ourselves what is happening every day to feed animals at zoos, what happens on dairy farms all the time, and what happens in the egg industry.

As we reflected on past employment, I recalled having a lamb named after me. I had visited a local farm to watch lambs being born, as part of a newspaper article I was writing. When it came to lambing season, perhaps inspired by Springwatch TV programmes, a farmer had thrown open her doors to people who wanted to see lambs being born. I spent a pleasant couple of hours on the farm in perfect spring sunshine and returned later that evening to watch a ewe giving birth. It was emotional and beautiful to watch. Because it was my birthday, they named one of the lambs Caroline.

I wrote my article and we published pictures of cute lambs gambolling in the sunny fields. The only vegan in the office was used to this kind of thing. She must have been so frustrated. There was a tiny piece of me that realised these animals were going to be slaughtered really quite soon. The rest of the brain decided I didn't want to know, didn't want to dwell on it, didn't want to use up emotional energy worrying about that.

I didn't make the connection. I wonder what questions I would ask now. How do you feel when you have to send these lambs to slaughter? How old are the lambs when they are killed? Does the mother react? What method do you use?

How does it sit with you — you clearly care about them and keep them well — but ultimately they are killed just because people like it on a plate with a bit of mint sauce?

I don't know what happened to Caroline, but I can guess.

In other newspaper articles, I talked to dairy farmers and saw calves tethered in pods, never stopping to ask why they were separated from their mothers at such a young age. I interviewed a pig farmer who was keen to teach children where their food came from. Maybe I should have suggested that he show the children around the abattoir.

My sister was for a while engaged to a butcher, who could bring home free or cheap meat every night. How ironic that a few years later, Nicola and her husband would go vegetarian. Just like me, at the time, she didn't think she could ever be vegan.

They often met up with another couple who were probably two of the first vegans in Jersey. She recalls asking them the same sort of questions as people still ask now… What's wrong with wearing wool? How does drinking milk cause any harm? She went vegetarian by phasing out meat and fish over the course of a year. Ditching the Christmas turkey was the final step.

Then she started reading up about the dairy industry, well before the days of the internet, and was disturbed enough to suggest a New Year resolution to turn vegan. They phased out dairy and eggs quite quickly after that and they have been vegan for more than 25 years.

She has three sons, two of whom have been vegan their entire lives. When they hit teenage years we thought that the greatest rebellion for them, rather than smoking or getting pissed on cheap beer, would be creeping into a McDonald's to order a Big Mac with extra cheese.

Back in the 80s, there weren't the vegan products we have now. The resolve of my sister and brother-in-law must have been even greater than mine is now. The soya milk wasn't as nice, and they had TVP, dried soya mince which they had to soak to rehydrate. Not exactly tempting.

Eating out was a minefield. Office parties and birthday celebrations, she tells me, were 'interesting', with some chefs making the effort to create something tasty with advance notice and others giving them a boring plate of steamed vegetables.

'It has improved a lot since then, though we sometimes still get the same questions as 30 years ago when people see you ordering something different or off-menu,' she says. 'I explain it from a personal angle to minimise the defensiveness that can ensue. My explanation is simple — for my health, for the animals, for the environment.'

It turns out I'm just as much of an eco-warrior as my sister is. I'm proud to be vegan.

I wasn't expecting that when I was at school, when I chose to do Communication Studies at college, or when I was a journalist. I wasn't expecting that when I became a charity worker. And I certainly wasn't expecting it to be the result of a six-month 'grown-up gap year'. But now, looking back, I feel that all the paths in my life, all the things I have done, all the decisions I have had to make, have led to this point. Before we set off, I secured a new job working for a charity which assists people with a disability or long-term health condition gain and maintain employment. It sits very well with me, as another pointer on my moral compass is inclusion.

The journey through India was about to change our lives, not in any overnight dramatic fashion, but step by step, over the next three months.

Rice between your cheeks

*'Somewhere, a long way away, people are doing
sensible things like mowing lawns and digging gardens'*
—*Michael Palin*

Day 66. Finally, we were in India. I was half-expecting
David to kiss the ground. 'The Pope did that. I can understand why,' he says, welling up. Again. Everything so far
had just been the prelude, the warm-up. Here, at last, was the
main event, our beloved India.

The journey from Colombo to Madurai alone introduced
us to many of the joys and challenges of the country. First, we
had to get out of Sri Lanka, spending way too long in the
interminable emigration queue. Indian women have mastered
the art of pushing in. We watched in fascination at first, but
when we realised that so many were taking advantage that we
might never reach the Customs officer, we got a bit feisty.
Well, I did. When one older woman pushed past, trying to
catch up with her husband, I had a go at her for pushing in and
being 'bloody rude'. I think it came out louder than I intended.

Another woman tried justifying her pushing-in because
she had a baby but I was so fed up that I stood my ground.

My full-length rainbow-coloured umbrella, which I had used as protection against the sun as much as the rain, was coming in handy as I positioned it to prevent her legs gaining ground. She was so far in my personal space that she was pinned up against me, leading me to keep my hands over my pockets.

The gate system at Colombo airport was the craziest we had seen. We went off to the shops and cafés and all was well, that is until the flight was boarding at the gate. Then there was a mad scrabble of people trying to board through one security point which we still had to get through before reaching our departure gate. It happened to be the same security point for the Chennai and Delhi flights which were boarding at the same time.

Staff from the other airlines were very good at calling forward their passengers, even though our flight had an earlier departure time. This meant that our queue was bombarded by people jostling to get through security, all of us pretty stressed, especially the handful of foreigners.

Eventually, after sitting on the twin-prop Bombardier for half an hour in the midday heat with no air conditioning, we were off on our 50-minute flight to Madurai.

We needed an ATM but the one at the airport didn't work. Or at least it didn't work for us. Little did we know that this was something that would frustrate us for the next three months. Fortunately, we were carrying just enough Indian rupees to pay for a taxi. The old driver had amazing ear hair and drove barefoot. The ancient car had dodgy steering and no seat belts. I was never sure why the taxi drivers wore white trousers and white shirt. They didn't wash very well.

It was a fabulous drive in to the city. Dirty, grubby, sweaty, hectic India, here we come.

Even though he was given an address and a map, the driver had to stop and ask for directions several times. On reflection, maybe neither was of any use. He was probably illiterate and he clearly needed reading glasses. Thankfully he squinted at his phone enough to bring a phone number into focus and he called our Airbnb. We got there in the end, down a small residential street, a dusty dead-end road. Fabulous. If this was as good as Hanoi, we'd be happy.

Our hosts welcomed us with sweet tea and water, and a good chat (I mean conversation, not the savoury snack). Having dumped our bags, we needed to get out and eat. We were sent on our way towards an ATM and a vegetarian restaurant. We found the restaurant easily enough. It was what I would describe generously as 'very local', which also meant that it took only cash, which we still didn't have. All the ATMs were at the other side of an exceptionally busy main road. The traffic here didn't seem to 'give' like it did in Vietnam. There was no second guessing it. But somehow we did it, usually by dropping in behind a local. If they went for it, we were their shadows.

As darkness fell, we found a branch of the Bank of India. The ATM was closed, but the bank itself was open, by which I mean you could squeeze in the doorway which was half-locked with chains at shoulder level. A woman gave me a smile that gave me false hope. She said the ATM would reopen very soon. The money was just being counted and the machine refilled. We waited outside and as soon as the shutters went up, in walked several men from the street, right in front of us like we were invisible. This was something else that we would have to get used to in the coming months.

David put his card in. It took several attempts to realise that, unlike back home, you are supposed to put it in, take it out straight away and then do your transaction. Oh no, panic, he told me the machine had swallowed his card. We located the ATM manager who opened the machine. He was a bizarre combination of perplexed and not that bothered. After about 15 minutes, David happened to look in his wallet and realised he had taken his card and already had it safely tucked away. Oops! He nudged me and, while the ATM man was still digging around the depths of the internal mechanism of the machine, David pretended that his card had just come back out of the slot... which confused the ATM manager no end.

Finally, we had 10,000 rupees, which meant we could eat. Back at the restaurant, that was where the fun really started. By now we were desperate for food and a cold drink.

The woman at the entrance kept saying to us: 'Juice.'

'Food,' we said.

'Juice.'

'Food.'

'Juice.'

'Food.'

Eventually we were ushered to sit down at a grubby table. It might have been yellow in a previous life. Five people, maybe members of staff, surrounded us. They could speak remarkably little English. They tried to take an order but no one seemed to know quite what was going on. It seemed to be unheard of for western people to come here and order, er, food.

A very grumpy chef came out and tried speaking to us. No luck there. I mean, it doesn't matter how many times you say it in Tamil, if I didn't understand it the first time, it just isn't going to happen. At some point they realised they could offer us a menu. Ah, good idea. Didn't realise you had a menu. Enough of it was in odd English for us to place an order.

An older man came over and said he could speak some English. And so we needed to re-order. I opened the menu and pointed at what I wanted. The man zoomed in to peer at it at a distance of 2 cm, at which point I got the giggles.

When our order started arriving at the table, Sprite became Fanta. A second Coke seemed out of the question so that became a Fanta too. Remarkably, the food was ok. Vegetable rice, garlic mushroom masala, another mushroom curry thing and naan. It was, however, pretty spicy which made us eat slowly and made us feel full quickly. The man kept popping by to practise his English, which really was not good enough to sustain conversation, much as I tried.

'Where you from?' he asked.

'England,' I ventured. (I wasn't going to try the whole 'Jersey in the Channel Islands' thing now.)

'English – you speak sweet English, the best,' he said.

'The Queen's English,' I replied. 'Thank you,' he said.

Surreal. And the bill? 360 rupees. Less than £4. Yes, we were going to love India.

The highlight of anyone's visit to Madurai is the Meenakshi Amman temple, the colourful towers dominating the city. We certainly did it justice, visiting first thing in the morning and going back in the evening for the ceremony which happens every day. Or does it? We had so much conflicting advice. Some said it happens every day at 9 pm. Others said it was every day except Friday, when it would be 9.30. Others said it was not every day, maybe only a smaller version might take place.

Luckily, with several evenings to choose from, time was on our side. On a Friday evening, we cleared the strict security measures and deposited our phones, cameras, shoes and bags. It's actually very liberating to walk barefoot around a place of worship, or anywhere for that matter, armed only with your reading glasses and a bit of petty cash. A couple from Australia who had a guide (we were the only white people around) told us that apparently the start time depended a bit on the alignment of the stars and it was up to the Brahmin to decide. Eventually the bells rang to signify the start at 10 pm. Some stars must have lined up at last.

Out of the inner sanctum burst a fast-moving crowd of worshippers led by Brahmin carrying a small silver chariot on their bare shoulders. I was never quite sure why they could bare their shoulders, chests and knees but no one else could. They made a lot of noise, armed with a long clarinet-like thing, a drum and bells, they carried fire on forks and created a lot of smoke. A lot. If it was incense I didn't really smell it. They walked around the shrines making as much racket as they could before going in the inner sanctum.

God knows what Shiva would make of it.

We were told all about Shiva on an excellent Storytrails walking tour of the city. In three hours my attention span didn't waver, but please don't ask me to repeat it all. Our guide Swarna told us about the 33 million gods in Hinduism, how Shiva is the destroyer and likes to dance, and that he married Meenakshi, who had three breasts. It is astonishing what the Indians will worship. It's also astonishing how little historical detail I recall.

We passed the statue of Nandi, a bull. 'How do you think Indians got around in those days?' asked Swarna. 'Tuk-tuk,'

David guessed, enjoying the way he could make our young guide laugh.

No, the bull was Shiva's steed. Nandi tried to get in the way when some intruder was around, interrupting something or other, and to this day if you are in the way, Indians will say: 'Don't be a Nandi.'

Some days we would head out and deliberately have no plan. We did that for a couple of hours in Madurai, not consulting our map app and not knowing where we were. Smiling children in smart school uniforms always said hello; we saw many cows in the street – I saw one tethered while a woman put a plastic bag behind it and collected the dung directly; there was nowhere to find a cold air-conditioned café; nowhere to buy toilet paper (we resorted to taking paper napkins from restaurants); there were small temples and icons everywhere; and women in orange hi-vis jackets over their saris were sweeping dust and rubbish, which meant that it was surprisingly litter-free. It was distressing, however, to see live chickens tied up on the back of a motorbike, and there were plenty of flies on the fish in the busy food market.

We stopped at a pharmacy to buy toothpaste, razors and mossie cream. The man wasn't particularly helpful. Each time he picked something up he smacked it with the other hand and a plume of dust bounced back into the air, and then he slapped it down on the counter. Boots it was not. And he didn't sell toilet paper or tissues.

The great thing about staying in an Airbnb is seeing how locals live – inside the home and out in the neighbourhood. Breakfast wasn't included, but we could help ourselves to tea and coffee in the kitchen, where the sink was old-fashioned and black with years of grime. We could often hear a dog barking and it turned out to be the family pet, living in a cage at the back of the house. Beryl was an old grey boxer with a tumour on her tummy. She had a bowl of rice, a bowl of water, a bit of poo which she was now pacing in, and she was obviously bored and distressed. I asked the older son, back from university for the weekend, whether we could say hello to her. We could, but no more interaction was encouraged. I didn't feel like I could say much. The son didn't offer to let her out. Pet dogs don't get walked like we walk ours at home. How assertive can you be as a guest of the family? Not very, it would seem.

So far on this journey we had been pretty lucky to find quirky cafés and reasonable restaurants, many of which catered to the tourist trade. They were never hard to find. In Madurai, however, the choice was only local and always ridiculously cheap. We were paying about £2 at mealtimes – the total bill for us both. But that usually meant that you didn't want to look too closely at your surroundings. When we stopped at one place for a small lunch, it was only after we finished that the cockroach crawled over my foot.

I liked the fact that we were finding places that played local music, not Justin Bieber and Ed Sheeran. Often, we'd see a staff member going around making whorls of smoke under pictures of gods on the walls. It was just as well they didn't have smoke alarms.

The first rule of Indian eateries is that whatever you first ask for will not be available. At the bakery where people were drinking chai, we asked for a black coffee. We were told we would have to go across the road to the corner shop for that. The stall which had pictures of pizza and the words 'Pizza' emblazoned across the front served only dosas and vadas. Every time a waiter declined with a wobble of the head, David got increasingly sarcastic. 'No, I thought not. I was only joking.'

And, of course, Indians eat with their hands. At several restaurants we visited there were no toilets, but there were basins for washing your hands before and after your meal.

It was amazing to watch people eat a meal with no knife or fork. They dunked their idlis, folded their dosas and scrunched up rice in a ball, all with their right hand. The left hand, of course, is for something else entirely. As David said, you've got to be careful you don't confuse the two because you don't want rice between your cheeks.

Be the change that you wish to see in the world

'Do the best you can until you know better. Then when you know better, do better'

—*Maya Angelou*

We had always aimed at stopping in Kerala for at least two weeks in a deliberate attempt to slow down and get under the skin of a place a bit more than three nights would achieve. From Madurai we went via Munnar in the hills to Alleppey for 14 nights and on to Fort Kochi. I had really hoped that, at some point, we would be able to lie on a beach on the west coast of India and just chill. In Alleppey here was our chance, we thought, and we were just about within walking distance of the beach.

First impressions were not good. We were shocked at the state of the main stretch of sand. A tide-line of rubbish had accumulated opposite the cafés and small restaurants, but litter was also scattered randomly as far as the eye could see. It was only after chatting to several people that we realised that much of the mess was caused by the summer's exceptional floods. A lot of people's possessions had been washed out to sea and the sea had spewed much of it back on the beach.

Well, we thought, we clean beaches back home. We carry bags to collect litter on our dog-walks wherever we go. Why not here? Time was on our side. To be honest, once you have been on a houseboat on the backwaters, there isn't much more to do in Alleppey. We became regulars at our nearest supermarket, which was surprisingly modern, and then, armed with a roll of 15 bin liners, we headed back to the beach. At 9 am on a blisteringly hot day (wasn't it always?) we started our beach clean. Having joined the beach at its most popular entry point, we headed north from the ruins of the pier, we reckoned less than 1 km. This was not a resort beach and it didn't really come to life with locals until the evening, so there weren't many people around. However, we were soon joined by a young man called Jibin who mucked in and happily helped us fill bag after bag of rubbish. There was a lot of glass. Dozens of Kingfisher beer bottles quickly filled a large sturdy sack. There was some obvious 'new' beach rubbish, things like ice cream containers, plastic spoons and crisp packets. But there were also a lot of shoes and flip-flops, medicine bottles, toothpaste tubes, nappies, handkerchiefs, the remains of a television set. God knows what stories lay behind each one.

Another man came up to thank us, he took photos and said he would bring up the matter of beach cleaning with the paid staff around here. We had noticed a team of women who rearranged the sand and fallen leaves at the roadside but they never ventured on to the beach itself. It annoyed us that it really would not take much effort to clean up if the tourism-related businesses — all the cafés, restaurants, ice cream sellers and watersport operators — got involved and spared a couple of hours in the morning while it is cooler to get their immediate area clean, and then keep it that way.

We dragged the bags up the beach and deposited them where a mound of rubbish was smouldering. As we did so, another man joined in to help us. It was a small but welcome contribution. It was a shame that the four young men who played cricket nearby did not do the same.

We thanked Jibin by buying him a drink and an ice cream and we sat on a wall in the shade for a chat. As he was showing me a map of India on his phone and recommending places to visit, I decided to show him where Jersey is, our beautiful island where the coastline is mostly unspoilt and the beaches are clean. A population of 100,000 and an area of 72 sq km (nine miles by five is the easier way of saying it) is difficult to comprehend here. And then he said something so simple and unexpected.

'You have a small island, but a very big heart.'

Before we had reached Kerala, we had wondered whether there was any practical way that we could help people with the clear-up. Once we were there, it was quite difficult to establish how we could be much use. So we simply took matters in our own hands and treated a beach clean as doing our bit. We bought more bin liners and headed back to the beach a second time but this time we nearly caused a diplomatic incident.

I was filling my first bin bag of the day when I noticed one of the cleaning ladies heading my way. David was joined by a man who came over out of curiosity while he was waiting for his vehicle to be repaired, and I was joined by a hippyish Indian called Sree, who was dressed in a bright T-shirt and baggy trousers, both of which must have been his favourites for the last 20 years. He put his hands together to thank us for what we were doing.

Six very stern-looking cleaning ladies gathered round. They were equipped with plastic baskets with holes in the bottom for the sand to filter out. They are keen to recycle things, especially plastic, so as to make a bit of extra money. We encouraged Sree to translate that we did not wish to offend and that we were here to help. We had stopped working in order to talk things through and it took quite a bit of effort and translation to win them around. Eventually there were smiles all round.

While we were talking, a bank of black cloud came over and the heavens opened so we headed to a tea stall. Sree talked and talked about how he wanted to better educate people about the environment. We chatted about life in India, religion, wealth, everything really. At one point I referred to poor people. 'How are you measuring "poor"?' he asked, prompting a conversation about how we cannot measure poverty only in terms of money. It was the kind of conversation that you don't want to end. I made a mental note of how pleasant it was not to have to rush somewhere else. To make the day perfect, we made friends with a black and white dog and her two puppies and gave them some biscuits. The café owner looked at us like we were crazy.

And, as we were about to leave, the cleaning team turned up in colourful clean saris, having knocked off work and changed out of their working clothes. We were happy to oblige with their requests for selfies with us.

Kerala is a dry state but you can find alcohol if you need it. That evening, we found a decent hotel with a restaurant and treated ourselves to only the third bottle of wine in 80 days.

Exploring the backwaters by kettuvallam and kayak hit home just how terrifying the floods must have been. In August 2018 nearly 500 people died in Kerala from the worst monsoon floods and landslides in a century. We nearly abandoned the idea of going there, as hundreds of others would have done. Our Airbnb host said that all forward bookings at her place had cancelled. When the floods came, her property was safe but she was inundated with calls for help and she accommodated ten relatives who needed a place to stay.

We were delivered to the kettuvallam (a houseboat) by Sunny, the short-sighted and hard of hearing tuk-tuk driver. He was a friend of our host, who explained that he made only short journeys in daylight due to his failing eye-sight. Even his tuk-tuk was dilapidated. The horn, an essential bit of kit in India, sounded like an underwater duck fart.

As we sailed through the backwaters, we could see that simple houses were built on a ridge between the waterway and the paddy fields beyond. People were walking on pathways less than a metre wide and only about 30 cm above the water level. We couldn't imagine what it was like for that water to be rising. There was simply nowhere for people to run to. It was difficult to comprehend how, after the deluge, they began to work out where their next meal and their drinking water supply was going to come from.

The community was going about its normal business. The water is where they bathe, shave, wash hair, wash dishes, do their laundry. I wondered which of the people we saw had lost someone they loved and how they were still coming to terms with that while still surrounded by water.

As the houseboat went along one waterway, all we could see on one side was mud. It should have been fields of rice. The crop was ruined. The other side of the waterway was still under water, with electricity pylons — indicating where the road should be — up to their knees in water. In the town, the canals which run alongside the main roads were where it was most obvious that a disaster had struck. Trees which had fallen across the canals and pulled down power cables had yet to be cleared away — the priority had to be homes and roads. The canals were clogged with mud and thousands of plants had taken the chance to grow there, making them a carpet of green.

Before we left Kerala, we chose to visit Kainakary, one of the small towns worst hit.

We didn't have a guide or anyone to introduce us but our friendly tuk-tuk driver Binesh pointed us in the direction of a man and his shikara. Knowing how hard this area had been hit, we didn't even try to haggle over the named price for two hours. We really only fancied one hour but felt we couldn't deprive him of the work.

One minute we were staring out at idyllic scenes, lilac water hyacinths dotting the water, palm trees swaying in the breeze, blue sky broken up a little with fluffy white clouds, keeping an eye out for kingfishers, herons, egrets and wood-peckers. And the next minute, our attention would be back to the harsh reality of life so close to the water. Banks stacked with sandbags, a half-submerged houseboat, paddy fields still choked with mud and stagnant water, a Red Cross mobile medical centre.

Our boatman told us that in the immediate aftermath of the floods, people were housed in temples, churches, schools and hospitals in Alleppey. Only recently had they returned to assess the damage to their homes. Many had lost every-thing. A narrow boat passed by with four large black plastic barrels balanced in the middle. It was the daily delivery of drinking water.

An old man paddled by. He splashed water onto the fish which were loose on the bottom of his boat, to keep them as fresh as possible. They were tiny. How was everyone surviving on such meagre food supplies? You wouldn't want to eat anything touched by this water, let alone wash your dishes and brush your teeth in it.

My Lonely Planet book referred to the fact that the backwaters are often so busy with houseboats that there can be gridlock. There was no chance of that while we were there.

One thing that the community did need to do was rally around and tackle the rubbish in the canals, particularly plastic bottles. Once again, I found myself reasoning that if every boat owner did one extra journey at the end of the day and cleared his area, they would be on top of it. Even as I thought it, I knew that many people had much more fundamental issues to deal with first — getting through each day as they rebuilt their homes and worked out where their next meal was coming from. But India is not short of spare people and there were plenty whose livelihood depends on tourism who had some free time to be proactive. The backwaters extend to a network of 1,500 km of canals, 38 rivers and five big lakes. If the whole area's tourism had been hit, there would be hundreds, if not thousands, of people who could do a concerted clean-up.

Mornings followed a similar pattern. We would be woken very early by the roosters in the garden (one was typical 'cock-a-doodle-do', the other was more in reply, hesitant and unsure) and then, just as we dozed off, a mullah started chanting. David muttered: 'Remind me never to get a chicken… Or a mullah.'

Initially, breakfast was adventurous. Our Airbnb host, Madhu, proudly offered us a different Keralan dish every morning. Soon we found ourselves dreading it. Sloppy, spicy curry was great at dinner and ok at lunchtime but, we found, difficult to face first thing in the morning. Most of the dishes were perfectly edible, apart from what we fondly referred to as idli-shit — just not for breakfast. Boiled egg curry, fish curry, onion crepe with lentil dal stuff, chickpea curry, spicy curried tapioca (nice taste, shame about the texture), and a dozen different ways to serve rice which seemed to get drier and more powdery every day. How we yearned for fried egg on toast, at a time when we still ate eggs.

Early in our stay, Madhu offered to cook us Keralan fish curry and, more importantly, she would show me how she did it. We chatted in her kitchen as she prepared everything from scratch, including soaking rice and grinding coriander. Nothing came out of a packet. She explained how she shopped at the small stores in the market street and grew her own tomatoes and cucumber. She didn't weigh anything and she didn't have any cookery books. The recipe, handed down by her mother, included lots of different spices, including turmeric, aniseed and cloves, but she was wary of putting in too much for us. The curry for her and her husband had been marinating for hours, already ten times stronger than ours. When she tasted the food, she simply poured a little on the palm of her hand and licked it.

All in all, we were in her kitchen for the best part of two hours, during which time she asked about our eating habits. To be honest, my life had been so busy that it was summed up by: cereal at breakfast, sandwich lunch and, for tea, whatever I could create from something in the cupboard or the freezer within ten minutes of thinking about it, or get a takeaway. Our eating habits, however, were changing fast. At this point, we knew that we were more determined than ever to make lasting changes to the way we ate when we got home, not least being vegetarian.

Towards the end of our stay, I wanted to thank Madhu for her kindness by buying a bunch of flowers but I couldn't find anything like a florist so instead we bought some spices. The street seller made us sniff and taste everything, crushing and rubbing spices to get the best aroma out of them. Having committed to buying some black peppercorns and cloves, we were keen to get going. Well, David was, but the packaging process turned out to be like a Love Actually scene, the one where Rowan Atkinson wraps a gift in a department store. The spices were poured lovingly into a plastic bag, then the man carefully got out a candle and lit it, then he gently folded the bag and sealed it by melting the plastic. He wasn't quite finished. He had to trim down the plastic bag. The only thing that was missing was a flourish with a pink ribbon.

We knew that sooner or later we might bump into some kind of festival in India. After all, with 33 million gods to play with, there was bound to be something that fell within our three months in the country. We had no idea that 21 September was going to be one of them.

We set off for what can only be described as a very random walk. Having visited the International Coir Museum slightly out of town, we decided to walk in the vague direction of the backwaters.

'You're never far away from a tuk-tuk,' I observed confidently, thinking that once we were hot and sweaty and ready to go back to Alleppey, we would be able to hitch a ride quite quickly. I was starting to realise that actually we hadn't seen a tuk-tuk for about half an hour. We were still relatively fresh, but with little clue as to where we were. It is very handy that many shopfronts in India have the full address in English on their sign boards, but we had left behind the last town that had done that, and now we were in territory where the few sign boards we saw were in the local language only. We decided not to resort to our map app just yet and continued walking. It didn't really matter where we were.

Everyone was so friendly, whether they were young or old, male or female, whether they came running to us, calling for a photo, or whether we had to smile first. They were, without fail, smiling back, waving or saying hello. It was all delightfully cheesy.

Then, about an hour into our walk, we stumbled upon some kind of ceremony. At first we assumed it was religious as there was chanting over a microphone and people were joining in. We passed by, keen not to disturb nor even to take photos, but as we drew level with it a number of the women gestured at us to join them. David sat on a chair at the back with the men. I noticed that the women seemed to be in a separate area, crosslegged on mats on the floor, so I sided with them, kneeling in the dust, before a lady found me a plastic chair.

We observed the ceremony politely and, after about half an hour of chanting, we stood to leave discreetly. But we were spotted. Four young men standing nearby insisted that we stay and eat. They said the food would be served in ten minutes. Actually, it felt like maybe they cut short the ceremony on our behalf, because suddenly everyone was standing up and getting us to come and sit at the table. We were served first, given a healthy serving of watery rice, a mildly spicy potato and vegetable combination and a small amount of sauce to go with it. It was surprisingly good. Everyone else ate with their fingers, but from somewhere they rustled up two spoons for us. The man next to me didn't speak any English, but other people came over and explained that they were remembering the social reformer Sree Narayana Guru Janthi, who died on 20 September 1928. A little research later informed us that he emphasised the motto of 'one caste, one religion and one god'. Community feasts and prayers are two of the things that happen around India on 21 September and we had stumbled upon them right here in... Oh, where were we? We asked the helpful lady who had insisted we stop by in the first place. Aryad North, we were told.

The servers came around with plenty more food, which we declined. It was lovely but we had had enough and we certainly didn't want to eat at the expense of anyone else. By now we had also had the chance to spot where the food had been prepared — outdoors in huge vats in accordance with the usual Indian food hygiene standards.

Dessert came in the form of fruit and a sort of muesli that looked like little larvae on a banana leaf. Even the people who began by just staring at us smiled broadly if we smiled at them. Or at least shake their heads which we took to be friendly. The Indian head shake, in which we were becoming quite proficient, has many purposes and we found ourselves adopting it even in conversation with each other. Many a time I would have to say to David: 'Don't you shake your head at me.'

I think people divide quite easily into camps — those who happily strip off in the gym changing room and those who don't. I am a fully signed-up member of the latter. But one day I found myself sitting on a plastic stool, in just my pants, otherwise naked in front of a petite young Indian masseuse, who parted my legs so that she could stand in front of me to rub a lot of oil in my hair.

It could have been worse. (There is always a 'could have been worse'.) Thanks to three months on the road, my underwear was not at its best. I was relieved that I was not wearing the pair that had been stained by Red Tiger Balm which had treated an inconveniently placed mosquito bite. It looked like there had been a bad accident, something that Imodium could not hold back, if you see what I mean.

We were in a stark room, no soft music, no robes, no little glass of water. I was all ready for an Ayurvedic massage. We had quite literally come in off the street. It was not something we planned that morning and ideally I would have liked a shower, but it was not offered. It didn't matter. It was quite apparent that my masseuse had not taken a shower either.

As soon as she closed the door, she said: 'Change.' Bit harsh. And she waited, watching me, while I took everything off. It was certainly not a matter of being left alone to get up on to the massage table and cover yourself with a towel. I closed my eyes and tried to relax while she tugged at my hair and dug in with her fingers. If I could only ignore my nakedness, it was bliss. And then I lay face down on the massage bed. No hole for my face, just a tiny square brown cushion to put my head on. No towel on the massage table, no disposable paper cover. It was just me and the black plastic and the oil. Lots of body-temperature warm oil.

Relax, I told myself. Relax — but not too much. I had recently eaten a roast paneer curry, though I supposed that if I did release inappropriately the effect might have been dissipated quite quickly by the fan overhead which was set on full blast. And then I remembered that she could probably see the mosquito bites on my cheeks and the associated pin-pricks surrounding them where the bug clearly had many stabs at it before success. The top-to-toe massage itself was very good. A bit of slapping and chopping and a lot of rubbing. Heck, she even fingered my coccyx and circled my buttocks. Then she flipped me over. Nothing to hide now.

The second she finished, she said: 'That's it, done.' No small talk. No 'lie there for a moment or two'. No dinging of a bell to bring you back into the room.

Oh, but we were not quite finished. She needed me to sit up, squelching in oil, and instead of handing me a towel, she insisted on rubbing me down with a piece of cloth not much bigger than a flannel. It looked like a mechanic's rag by the time she had mopped up the oil and a layer of Indian dust.

'Nice time in Kerala, ma'am?' as she lifted a boob to wipe underneath.

Early on in our two weeks in Alleppey, we walked past a small tea shack at the side of the road. We both thought the same thing — we should go in there before we moved on in our travels. One day, as we walked back past it on the way 'home', we heard the man call over to us. 'Coffee?'

We couldn't resist. It was quite dark, a single dull bare bulb in the middle of the ceiling, wooden tables and plastic chairs. Four old men were sitting in there, one was tucking in to a plate of rice with his fingers, others just had a small coffee or chai in front of them. They were of a generation who don't speak much English and they didn't try for any conversation, with us or each other. Our host did try, however, even though he too had limited English beyond 'Where are you from?' While he got on with his brewing, we sat and chatted. David couldn't wait to find out what the 'free gift' was with the packet of incense sticks we had just bought. It turned out to be a small packet of matches which we did not need so we offered them to our host. He was delighted. He refused to accept payment for David's glass of coffee.

The next day, the shack looked closed but the man spotted us and welcomed us in anyway. He insisted on preparing two glasses of black tea and we established that his name was Nazeer. While the kettle was on, he insisted we take photos. First, though, he put on a better shirt and popped round the back to get his hat. He was poor as poor could be but he was proud of what he did. There was something dignified about him, even just the way he poured coffee between two stainless steel jugs. He started talking about a son and grandson. With limited English, he seemed to be asking for 3,000 rupees. We were not exactly sure what for.

'So your son is in France…?' David ventured.

'Yes. Closed Sunday. Holiday,' he said.

He then invited us to the room behind his shack, where his 90-year-old mother-in-law was sitting on a bed. Pulling out an old biscuit tin, he showed us receipts for various medical treatment. We had already noticed that his left foot was bandaged. He still insisted that we didn't pay for our tea.

We walked away feeling that, regardless of how he would spend it, we could easily give him 3,000 rupees. It wouldn't mean much to us but it would make a huge difference to him, considering he charged about 10 rupees for a cup of coffee. We said we would be back before we left Alleppey.

Actually, we visited several times. We met his wife, Sheeja, and his son, Rishan. The first time we saw Rishan, he was playing in the dirt in the tiny yard, with an old plastic tub and a spoon. That was when we decided that we needed to go back to the handy supermarket just down the road and, when we stocked up on crisps and bananas, we also bought pens and paper for the lad. A couple of days later, Sheeja was so happy and so proud to show us Rishan's drawings in his exercise book. She gave us the most delicious warm egg vadas and some kind of deep-fried egg doughnut.

On our last day in the town, we sat in Nazeer's shack, very sad to be saying goodbye. We left an envelope with them. I seem to have recounted this story like it was the most natural thing in the world for me to give away money. It is not. David is the one who would give the shirt on his back without a care in the world. On this occasion, we both agreed immediately that there was no harm in helping Nazeer. Even if he tried to ask for money from every white person who passed by (though this was not a touristy area and even less so after the floods), didn't he need it more than we did? What we gave him was less than the price of a Chinese takeaway back home.

After our last free drink in the tea shack, I had a great big hug with Sheeja and we waved back, smiling all the way down the street.

By the time we reached Kerala, we were definitely used to rock-hard beds, mosquitoes spoiling any chance of sitting in a garden in the evening, and dribbly tepid showers, if we were lucky. The shower in Alleppey was predictably disappointing. Our host told us that if we required hot water, there was a tap in the garden — the water there was heated by solar power and was what we described as scorchy-hot. If we wanted a bath, she could lend us a bucket.

We noticed that a cage was being built in the garden. We asked what it was for. We're getting a dog, she said excitedly. A dachshund puppy was due any day. The cage was going to be raised off the ground so that rats couldn't get him. Oh, dear God. We tried as best we could to say how we look after dogs in the west, expressing hope that the puppy would have lots of love and attention and be allowed in the house. We left before he arrived, but I thought about him for weeks.

We were getting used to expecting the unexpected. We headed to Fort Kochi, where we were looking forward to seeing the Chinese fishing nets. We hired bikes, we explored the touristy haunts of Jew Town, we pootled around with Abbas the tuk-tuk driver, and we saw a sign outside a shop which boasted that 'Lional' Blair had bought a suit there during the making of The Real Marigold Hotel. We found lovely cafés in the small town. It was outside one of them that we were approached by a well-dressed and good-looking young man who asked us if we fancied being in a film. We couldn't work out what the catch was, he didn't seem able to give us more detail, but we both concluded that he was talking about a part in a porn film.

'Yes, ok,' David said. 'But we're going to have a nice cup of tea first.'

Laughing, we ducked into the nearest café and went upstairs to indulge in Kit-Kat milkshakes, and from there we could see the street below and watch the man waiting. And waiting. Luckily, by the time we snuck out, he had gone.

Once again, the beaches in the area were sadly lacking. At one point we tried to get on the beach but were hampered by the fact that the army had taken over much of the coast and we passed signs saying: 'Shoot first. Shoot hard. Keep shooting.'

We took a ferry over to Broadway where we stumbled upon a fabulous fruit and veg market, where people were bustling around, carrying huge sacks or bowls on their heads. This was an area for wholesalers and there was one shop which evidently sold only bananas. I couldn't stop myself from asking if they had any apples. 'Can't take you anywhere,' David said. I gave him the Indian head wobble.

We headed to Lulu Mall, the biggest mall in Asia. It included branches of Marks and Spencer, McDonalds, Pizza Hut and Accessorize. Although we treated ourselves to a 'normal' pizza, we didn't really enjoy the brush with feeling western again and we felt like we were cheating.

We preferred a tiny vegan, organic café near our home-stay where we somehow talked ourselves into a yoga lesson. I had always fancied doing yoga in Kerala. What was I thinking? We had to get up ridiculously early and the instructor, Arush, picked us up and took us to his house, where we took the outside staircase to the roof. We are absolute beginners, as he was about to discover. It was only the two of us for an hour and we were put through our paces, stretching, posing and balancing. I hoped it wouldn't set off my occasional lower back issues. I'd been feeling slightly queasy and, when someone downstairs started cooking something in ghee, I also hoped I wouldn't vomit.

Arush asked us if we would like to try aerial yoga. We felt we should. I can't believe that David gave it a go. He squeezed into this bright green silk dangling from the ceiling and closed his eyes. At one point, while suspended upside down, he looked like he was wearing a Borat mankini. Our kids were never going to believe this photo when they saw it on Facebook.

We headed back to the fishing nets to see if we would catch them in action. It turned out that it was highly unlikely unless you're prepared to pay the fishermen to leap into action. We weren't.

We made a point of being nice to stray dogs on the beach. Those rabies jabs gave us a certain confidence and, besides, anyone who has any affection for dogs knows that a wagging tail is usually a good sign. Indians looked on in astonishment. While we sat around to watch the sun go down (not as romantic as it sounds, with the view of industrial Kochi to one side and crumbling promenade on the other), two men came up asking if we would be filmed to recommend their restaurant. We wondered if this was some kind of scam but couldn't work out what it was. We told them we had never been to the restaurant. That didn't deter them and they stuck a microphone in front of David, asking whether he had heard of the restaurant. 'No,' he said.

We were getting nowhere, the camera was turned off, and they gave us a business card in the vague hope that we might visit. David showed it to the friendly fat black labrador who had plonked himself next to us. The dog gingerly took it in his mouth and ate it.

Granny-ji farted in the back of the bus

'The human race should just slow down and think about what it is doing'

—*Michael Palin*

I am not sure why we trusted the woman at our hotel in Panaji, fresh out of the Little Hitler School of Hospitality, when she suggested we take a bus tour to get to know Goa. It was 250 rupees a head. It was only when I had paid it that I thought, gosh that's cheap, I wonder why.

She hadn't shown me the itinerary, she didn't tell me the name of the company or give me a receipt. She merely wrote a few place names on a scrap of paper. They included a couple of temples and churches in Old Goa which we wanted to visit.

We were picked up at 10 am. The bus was a pretty, old thing, its sides painted with peacocks. The door was held on by a piece of string. On the go, the bus creaked and threw out black fumes. Less pretty inside, where the seats had been covered with thick plastic, which generated even more sweat, which was considerable as there was no air conditioning. I mean, a tourist bus in India with no air conditioning. Unbelievable.

The guide, in his scruffy jeans and world-weary sandals, was helpful in accommodating us two westerners. Everyone else was Indian so he spoke to them, a lot, in Hindi. He handed us a piece of paper with the itinerary. We were with Express Travel Agents & Tour Organisers — Approved by the Government of Goa. Most of the passengers couldn't speak any English, including a sweet old lady we shall call Granny-ji and her husband. She smiled at us often and after lunch gestured for me to sit next to her on a wall, which I did until I noticed the large ants dangerously close to my pants.

So, this was the chronological order of our tour stops. It was just as well we always kept an open mind.

*Fun Science Museum. Remember, we told ourselves, low expectations. Surprisingly it was fun, a quirky mix of childhood games and magical illusions.

*Miramar, 'a lovely golden beach of soft sands, along Blue Arabian Sea'. We drove past it so fast I had no idea it was on the schedule until afterwards.

*Basilica of Bom Jesus, Old Goa. Nice to take a photo, some saint's remains are there.

*Se Cathedral, Old Goa. Nice to take a photo, the largest church in Asia.

*Shri Manguesh Temple. Average Hindu temple, ten minutes enough.

*Shri Shantadurga Temple. Average Hindu temple, ten minutes enough.

*Margao (Bypass). We went past it or around it and four people got off to catch their train to Mumbai, but why was it a feature on the itinerary? Not a clue.

*Colva Beach, longest beach in Goa. People swimming in jeans and shirts. No one in costumes or shorts. No one sitting on a beach towel. At least it was clean and we got an ice cream.

It was the three things that were not on the itinerary, however, that proved to be most memorable: a wax museum, an aquarium and a house of horrors, all of them utterly bizarre and only fit to be closed down. The wax museum in a scruffy old building included some random historical figures like Mozart and Einstein, as well as some Indian figures like Mother Teresa and Gandhi, whose birthday it was on the day of our visit. Initially we had an English-speaking guide provided to us, not that we asked for it. She didn't tell us anything that wasn't on the information boards. 'Gandhi,' she pointed. 'Gandhi.' They always said it twice. We were pleased when she suddenly seemed to have a better offer and off she went with no explanation. Thankfully the whole thing took only three minutes from start to finish. Madame Tussauds it was not.

On the way back from Colva Beach, we made one last stop at a very sad aquarium. One or two tanks contained just a single fish and nothing else — no rocks, no greenery, an albino terrapin with no place to get out and bask, one fish which looked like it had grown too big even to be able to turn around in the tank. I was getting angry. I wanted to say something. David didn't think there was much point. Our fellow passengers seemed enthralled. We exited past a revolting statue of a man in beach shorts holding a child. It was filthy. Surely no one even takes a photo next to this? We took a photo. There were similar things in the garden, women holding fish, a woman on a bridge gaily kicking her legs in the air. All surreal, in a bad way.

And then we were shown the house of horrors. In effect, our third that day. It was so basic it belonged to an eternity ago. It was enough to make us jump once or twice but there was no variation on a theme. It was just mechanised bodies moving towards us with a bit of screaming.

As we headed homeward bound feeling like we were in some parallel universe, Granny-ji, with her long grey hair, bright green sari and pink flip-flops, farted in the back of the bus. Indians have no worry about farts and belches in public places. There was the 'maid' at our last place in Alleppey who burped like an old man every two minutes. On the train there was a young man lying on the seat who was snorting a dry sniff every couple of minutes, and then he topped that with a fart for all to hear. Not a care in the world. Not a flinch. Didn't even open his eyes.

The road back to Panaji was bumpy, there was a lot of road-building going on. In some places the traffic-calming measures were sets of 20 small humps. It gave you what is known as an Indian massage. We worried that it might trigger more outbursts from Granny-ji.

It had been the kind of day that David needed a beer. A long cold beer.

Our hotel in Panaji was the Indian equivalent of Fawlty Towers. When we first arrived, we noticed that there were only about five sheets of toilet paper left on the roll. I asked three times, in person and on the phone. 'I'll send the boy,' was always the answer. The boy never arrived. I have never had to beg for toilet paper before, but finally it was handed over in reception on the fourth nagging.

Wifi had been difficult. At the end of the day of our odd tour, we asked if we could order some food from the room service menu and sit in the breakfast room, where the wifi signal was reasonable. No, the room service menu applied only to the room. We ordered noodles, a large Kingfisher beer and a lemonade. The food arrived — as a takeaway from somewhere over the road. We asked if we could continue sitting in the lobby, where there was a small table and, more importantly, the wifi. No.

Banished to our room, we realised that the beer was missing. I called reception. No beer? No, it was Gandhi's birthday — a dry day. Could we not have been told that when we placed the order? Apparently not. We felt hard done by that there was no offer of an alternative drink and sulked that there was no wifi in our room.

At breakfast the next morning, we were making use of the wifi connection, eyes down on screens, when we were vaguely aware of a woman saying 'Good morning, sir.' We didn't look up because we knew that two other guests had arrived.

'GOOD MORNING, SIR,' she repeated, at much greater volume, directed at David. It was enough to make a grown man stand up and take his hands out of his pockets. She was scary, that one. Each time we saw her she seemed to think she was in charge of telling us what to do (like that tour of South Goa). We weren't going to take her advice again.

Our three-star hotel certainly had the most comfortable (bug-free) bed we had had in many weeks, but the catering was most definitely lacking. We were not offered tea or coffee in the morning. One day I had successfully asked for cold milk to go with the cornflakes. It was the first time I had seen a cornflake in three months. It was still difficult to face idli and curry at 8 am.

The next day, however, no such luck. The boy scurried off to get some but came back empty-handed. 'Sorry, ma'am, we have no cold milk.' He stood there staring at a

cupboard for a bit and then stationed himself back in the
corner, standing and waiting. Suddenly, five minutes later,
he remembered that he also had an order for two black teas
and he had to leave the room again, only to return with two
teabags, and he put the kettle on.

Luckily, our second day in Panaji was taken up with exploring on our own and we found that we liked the place a
bit better — lots of old houses, a Portuguese influence, an
old quarter, a lovely church, and some cute cafés and cosy
restaurants.

On another day, we tried to find a beach to relax on. Where
there were open stretches of sand, there were no refreshments,
no toilets and no shade whatsoever. Frustrated, we walked
further along the beach until we saw what we thought was a
mirage. We spotted sun umbrellas, a garden and, most importantly, a bar. We had to scramble up over rocks and then climb
around a gate, holding on tight. It was sort of obvious that we
shouldn't be entering the premises this way but we had cold
beer in mind and we guessed that the colour of our skin and
our age would work to our advantage.

A member of staff spotted us and came over, saying that
we should go around to the front. Apologising profusely and
politely (we still had no idea where we were), we were
relieved when he accepted that we were genuine enough,
but really he should have insisted that we go through the
entrance where there was a security scanner, for it turned
out that we had gatecrashed a five-star international resort
hotel. We pulled up a couple of loungers at the poolside and
ordered a couple of blissfully cold beers. Best of all, we had
with us books and reading glasses. The waiter even moved

the parasol around to keep us in some semi-shade. The toilets were the best bit, a luxurious subterranean block of clean, western toilets. I could have stayed in there all day. We lay on our loungers, feeling smug and chilled, a tiny part of us wishing we were staying here. It was a cheap afternoon so we tipped the waiter handsomely.

The last time we had to lift our suitcases, on the train from Kochi to Goa, we realised that it was time to send a few items home to lighten the load. So we chose a day to go to the nearest Post Office. There was no queue at the Parcel Packaging Centre so we walked right up to it. Could we have this parcel packaged, please? No, we don't do that. Silly me, of course you don't.

We were directed to the back of the building, outside to the tiny Xerox shop behind the chapel. The man invited us in and we sat down. He didn't say much but he could see what we needed. He trotted off to the back room, returning with an old shoebox with no lid. He tried the things for size and prodded until our package squeezed in. It would do. He strapped a piece of paper on the top using string.

Next, the man got out his roll of gaffer tape. That's more like it, I'm thinking. But it was like he had never handled it before. The ends were all messy and twisted and at one point he taped down his hand. He picked up a piece of ragged muslin which he wrapped around the shoebox. I was slightly more reassured about the likelihood of my parcel getting home. But it turned out that he needed to apply a plastic window for the documents — proof of ID and a form to declare its contents. In order to do this, he needed to use a sewing machine, of course.

He retreated to the back room, giving us a chance to look around. It was what your great grandfather's shop would have looked like, there were stacks of old paper, some tied with string, on the floor and on random shelving. It had all accumulated a layer of dust and cobwebs like it belonged in an ancient attic. I felt sure he knew where everything was.

An older man came in. He stood in the entrance, looking like he had forgotten what he had come in for. He said a prayer.

The parcel-wrapper re-emerged but walked straight outside, muttering something. As if sensing our confusion, the new man explained that his friend was working with a second-hand sewing machine and something on it had broken, so he had gone next door. A customer came in and bought two brown envelopes. He helped himself from the shelf, paid and left. An older woman required the photo-copying service. The dusty photocopier (from the 1980s perhaps) actually worked. While she waited the electric fan scattered some papers to the floor.

The man who was holding the fort asked for a copy of our ID. I showed him a picture on my phone. He tried to copy it but each time he placed my phone on the photocopier the image turned from vertical to horizontal and he really couldn't get to grips with it. It only photocopied as a black screen. He was confident that David's driving licence would suffice for ID so he copied that instead.

Our man returned. Success! He had the muslin with a plastic window attached. Now all it needed was for the muslin to be wrapped around the box. The two men did this together. All the edges were finished the way we would fold wrapping paper but instead of using Sellotape they hand-sewed it in place with white cotton. It took forever. The men chatted happily without a care in the world, they felt no pressure to finish the task any faster than the time it took to complete. India, we were reminded, teaches you patience. Job done. 150 rupees (approximately £1.50), keeping someone in work and recycling materials to boot.

Now it was back to the Post Office. We reminded ourselves to count to ten. The man at the counter was none too happy that we didn't have our passports. I suggested I could email the image of my passport to him. We pointed out that Xerox man had told us that the driving licence would suffice. He repeated his request for a copy of the passport and I repeated my answer. This exchange continued three or four times, until he gave up. I won!

A queue started behind us. Inevitably the ripe old man immediately behind me was in my personal space, but I smiled and warned him we could be some time.

I guessed that I would not be able to pay for the postage by debit card, but I asked anyway. When he gave me the inevitable 'no', I just replied: 'No, I knew you wouldn't. I was just having fun. Cash it is.'

Finally, we walked out into the blazing midday sunshine. Sending a parcel back home had only taken two hours.

If we thought sending a parcel was arduous, booking a train took tedium to a whole new level. Although I suspected that booking a train in India might be difficult, I had hoped it was easier now that there is online booking. I had already tried booking online. I had wasted an hour on a flimsy internet connection. There were plenty of trains running — the problem lay in working out the details of where you were leaving from and where you were arriving — in terms of station name, not just city (it could be the difference between

arriving at Kings Cross, Paddington or Euston in London),
what class you wanted, and whether your choice of train
actually ran on a specific day.

I had tried emailing a company who had helped us in
Vietnam. Even they were flummoxed. 'If you impossible to
change the date you can directly to buy the ticket with IRCTC
website. We highly apologise for the inconvenience.'

We looked around for travel shops. There were usually
loads in a town when we were not looking for them. We
asked in Thomas Cook. We were clearly the first people to
have asked that question. They suggested some bloke 'round
the corner, next to Mustafa's' but they couldn't remember
his name.

Instead we crossed the road with the aim of ending up in
Quest Travel, though we were actually next door at the
Lokmanya Co-operative Society who, it turned out, booked
trains.

We were ushered to the first floor. There was a slight
whiff of toilet at the top of the stairs. A sign on the door
reminded users to flush. In the office, half a dozen balloons
were clinging to the wall with static, a couple of them
feeling a little deflated. Maybe someone had a birthday a
week ago. Also on the wall was a tiny Ganesh statue surrounded by half a dozen yellow marigolds and a lit incense
stick. A couple of wires dangled from the ceiling. A computer cable was taped to the edge of the customer-facing
desk. In places, it had given up holding the wire, but many
small strips of brown tape were still there.

We perched on light beige plastic chairs, which were
clean at the front but grubby underneath. There were three
young women in blue uniforms, one of them looking after
us. Any time they needed anything they summoned what we
could only assume was the new boy as they seemed to tease

him in good humour. We soon established that we needed to return the next day because the booking system for the trains would be released in the morning. I never really understood why the Indian rail system did this.

In true British fashion, we were at the office for 9.30. Actually we were there with ten minutes to spare, allowing us time to notice the dead dog on the street outside. She looked like she had gone peacefully, rather than being knocked down by traffic on the busy road nearby. Strangely, I felt relieved to see a dead dog rather than one which was badly injured.

In the office, the first question was whether we got the message from the hotel. No. (Didn't surprise us.) Luckily the message had not been vital, they wanted us to come along to the office anyway — but the schedules would not be out until 10.30.

We went away to have a drink in the nearest café, a lovely locals' place, chosen for its proximity, though it turned out that the coffee was perfectly drinkable.

At 10.30 we were back. We were informed of the price and David sat with cash in hand as if payment was imminent. A more senior man offered coffee. 'Yes, one please, black,' we said. Ten minutes later, one milky coffee and a carton of mango juice were produced with a smile.

Anyway, eventually, we had our train tickets in hand. Not quite what we wanted (Old Goa to CST, the historic main terminus in Mumbai) but near enough (Madgaon to LLT).

The commission for the agency? 40 rupees (about 50p) for two hours' customer time.

I moo'ed at a mullah

'Poverty is not an accident. Like slavery and apartheid, it is man-made and can be removed by the actions of human beings'

—Nelson Mandela

I sat in our hotel room in Mumbai, trying to work out its square area. I'm not very good at guessing measurements but let's just say that there was plenty of space to move around the double bed. We were back at our modest hotel after visiting the Dharavi slum and I was lying on the bed looking at the space I had for six nights. If this was an area in the Dharavi slum, it would be divided into two or three smaller units and likely accommodate two or three families of five or six.

It had been a mind-boggling day visiting the slum with Reality Tours & Travels. We chose them because they promote responsible tourism and put 80% of profits back into social programmes. They were running slum tours before the 2008 film Slumdog Millionaire came out. Slumdog may have been loved by millions of people around the world, but not in India. Here, they thought it portrayed the Dharavi slum only in a negative light — filth, squalor, dirt, crime. The term 'slumdog' itself was considered derogatory, suggesting that the residents here are the lowest of the low.

Reality Tours have a strict 'no photography' policy so as to preserve the dignity of people living and working in the slum. Admittedly, at first it felt very strange to have relegated cameras and phones to our rucksacks, but we agreed with their principle.

One million people live in an area of just two square kilometres. As we arrived, we could see some dull high-rise blocks of flats within the slum area called, with no hint of irony, Evershine Meadows.

Our tour started with a walk through the commercial district where Dharavi has its own vibrant economy. People were working in dark rooms in what to us looked like Dickensian conditions. Recycling is the biggest industry. Here, they recycle plastic bottles, they sort plastics into different colours before melting them down and selling off the new components. Fumes from burning plastics and paints are acrid. The heat in the semi-basement where bakers are churning out breads and biscuits is intense. Many immigrant workers arrive here, the City of Dreams, having left wives and children behind in rural areas and they work long hours in a dark dirty room. What shocked me most was hearing that they also sleep in the same place.

The hide-tanning area was distressing. Another penny dropped and I knew that I would never again buy leather. Most of the skins, from sheep and goats (not cows as they are sacred), feed the European and American market in the form of bags, purses and jackets.

In another area, potters were at their busiest, preparing for Diwali by producing thousands of little clay pots to hold candles, for sending around the country.

As we walked past the open sewer, our guide explained that sanitation was the biggest problem here. Very few homes have their own toilet. Some neighbourhoods have public facilities but the people have to pay each time. There were sleepy dogs and skinny cats. Surprisingly we saw only one rat and that was a dead one.

Some homes are made of concrete, others are more shanty with corrugated roofing. We walked down alleyways where the sun will never shine, alleys so narrow that they are one-person wide. No room for passing someone, you just have to wait, or give way to the man who is carrying a sack of concrete on his head. There was mud and rubbish on the floor, water pipes to trip you up and cables dangling overhead. A ragged piece of cloth serves as a front door. Electricity and water supplies are available but are often limited to certain times of day.

Some people are doing quite well. Those who arrived here first have a bit of extra space and many rent out upstairs rooms for a bit of extra income.

Women were washing clothes, scrubbing them on the floor, or cleaning out their stainless steel pots and pans. There were stern-looking barefoot children in grubby clothes, but there were also children in pristine school uniforms running around playing, laughing and saying hello.

Dharavi is Asia's largest slum and one of the densest populations in the world. 60% of Mumbai's residents are slum-dwellers, people who live illegally on land owned by the government.

This visit was certainly not about taking selfies in the squalor. It was much more about appreciating the fascinating economy of a city within a city. There are about 5,000 businesses and 15,000 single-room factories in Dharavi.

The slum is the most literate in India, with a literacy rate of almost 70%. Our guide said that people here are considered middle class — many men commute to work in other parts of the city. The poorest people in Mumbai are the ones who are homeless on the streets.

We were very aware that we could only just touch the surface of most of the places we visited, but Mumbai left an impression. Two other fascinating parts of life in the city were the dhobi ghats and the dabba-wallahs.

The ghats, built during the British Raj, are where all of Mumbai's commercial laundry goes. 7,000 people handle half a million items here each day. They pride themselves on not losing an item. All the hotels and restaurants send their sheets and table-cloths here.

The dabba-wallahs, about 5,000 of them, are the men who bring homemade lunches to the city. They collect them from homes beyond the city limits and bring them in on the train. They can be seen at a couple of stations, emerging to transfer the lunchboxes onto bicycles for delivery to offices. A mistake is made about once in six million deliveries, an incredibly successful operation.

Having enjoyed the film The Lunchbox, we wanted to see the dabba-wallahs for ourselves as they came through Churchgate Station. And it was opposite the entrance to the station that once again I found myself striking up a conversation with some street sellers. A young man had come by trying to sell colourful papier maché elephants on a string. Another had some purses and some peacock feathers. Millions of the feathers are sold across the country because the peacock is India's national bird.

Tourists will always be told that the feathers have naturally moulted, because that would be within the law. But it's not true. There are no legal peacock farms and these gorgeous showy birds are being killed for their feathers.

Each time I saw people selling feathers, I made a point of saying that they would look better on the peacock.

On the first day in Mumbai we wandered in the streets from our hotel. It was just a way of getting the feel of our local area and we put down the map once we got to the Colaba Causeway. I always like a good market and we soon found one, away from the traffic, selling fruit and vegetables. We then realised that it was not just fruit and veg, but also fish and chicken, which we could smell, particularly as there was no protection from the midday sun.

Everyone was friendly and full of smiles. A group of young children had made up a game by throwing a sandal and I guessed that it was a matter of each child trying to throw their flip-flop as close as possible to the first one, much like boules or pétanque. One little boy wearing just dirty white pants emerged from a building to pee against a motorbike (twice). We were amused by a man who was trying to brush cockroaches away from his property into the street. They kept turning around and running back in. Even he saw the funny side of it, as did a girl who was trying to help. One cockroach was flicked almost to the other side of the street where it was swiftly pecked on and eaten by a chicken. An older man was pedalling away on a static bicycle, the wheels turning a device to sharpen a knife.

The road turned to a lane, and the lane into an alleyway. Having walked through a residential area, we emerged at a harbour. Children were splashing about in the sea, jumping off steps, and two older boys were trying to catch fish with a large piece of fabric. On the rubbish-filled beach, right out in the open, a man was squatting to have a poo and splashing water between his legs.

A cow sanctuary at Bombay Panjrapole, a bit off the beaten track, seemed a good place to start the second day's explorations. We hopped in a taxi outside the hotel. We said hello to see how friendly the driver was. I often did this to determine how much English they could speak. He was a skinny old man dressed in a long white robe and cap. He also had a long white beard but no moustache. We asked Mohammed to take us to Bombay Panjrapole. He didn't understand. Bombay Panjrapole. I showed him the name written down, I repeated it but I wasn't getting anywhere. After a frustrating few minutes, I came up with a communication method that I thought couldn't fail.

'It's a cow sanctuary,' I said. 'Mooooooo.'

He let me moo again.

'Ah! Bombayyy Pange-ra-pollay,' he said. 'Yes. One cow, two cow. Bombay Panjrapole.'

Nevertheless he still had to stop a couple more times to ask directions (I like to think that he also moo-ed at the people he asked) and then I had to help a bit with the directions on my map app. He confessed that he had never been there in 37 years' taxi driving so he came in and had a look as well. Of course, I realised afterwards, he wasn't just interested in cows, he was hoping to get more driving from us.

'One cow, two cow. No, so many cows!' he chuckled. 'Hehe.'

His growly laugh was something akin to Steptoe's. We liked Mohammed enough to ask him to pick us up again at 5.30 pm as we wanted to go to the Royal Opera House for a night of jazz. He said that six o'clock would be better, using the excuse that the traffic would be (relatively) lighter and the temperature (marginally) lower. The truth was that it suited him better because he had mullah duties at his mosque.

At 6 pm we hopped in his taxi. 'Royal Opera House,' I said.

'Where?'

'Royal Opera House.' Surely every Mumbai taxi driver knows where the Royal Opera House is? It's been there for more than 100 years. He didn't understand. 'Which hotel?' he asked.

In exasperation, I looked at David to help me out. Nothing. I knew it was coming. If I can moo at a mullah, I can damn well do my Maria Callas impression and sing at him in a loud high pitch. (My singing is awful.) I even extended both arms within the confines of the small sweaty taxi to make my point. Three times. I tried showing him the map. 'It's near French Bridge,' I suggested.

'Ok, ok. What hotel?'

I showed him the map. At last, he said: 'Oh. Opera. Opera House. Yes yes. Hehe.'

I swear he was doing it on purpose.

It was bothering me. One simple orange crisp packet. It was nestling under a railing, stuck between the white rail and the green wooden boards of the deck of a boat.

We were heading towards Elephanta Island, about an hour and a half's journey from Mumbai. There was a family opposite us, mum and dad, a set of grandparents and two children, a girl of about eight and a boy of two. The children had been happily sharing a packet of crisps. I didn't think much more of it. The mum peeled a small orange and they shared it out. Without a thought, and without a care as to who might notice, she threw the peel over the side of the boat. Although it was not something that I would do, I reasoned that, ok, it's biodegradable and my mind wandered to other things.

There were dozens of commercial boats moored off the city's coast. There was an industrial stretch of coastline in the hazy distance. The noisy boat made a slow plodding progress towards the island. I noticed bits of rubbish floating in the sea. It was not as bad as I thought it might be, but still there was the occasional area where it was huddled together, presumably herded by some underwater current.

The girl was doing as her mother did. She picked off pith and threw it over the side like it was a game. Then I saw her tearing up a piece of white paper and sprinkling it over the side like confetti. Paper, I thought. At least it was not plastic.

The mum tried to throw a piece of paper overboard but it was light enough to be lifted by the wind straight back at her and back on the boat. She sort of shrugged her shoulders.

And then I spotted the crisp packet. It was sitting there under the railing. It was the one that the kids had been holding a short time before. I started willing it to stay where it was or to be carried by the wind further on to the deck. I would pick it up myself if it headed my way.

A passing boat caused a bit of wash and spray came up. The only person to get wet was the mother in her royal blue sari. She laughed it off but her seat was wet and she came and sat next to me, with her sleepy younger child dozing off on her shoulder. Karma, I thought.

And then I noticed that the crisp packet was not there any more. I shifted position to see if it was on the deck but I couldn't see it. I was quite perturbed that it had unnecessarily gone into the ocean. I wanted to say something. I wanted to nudge the grandfather, who was next to me earlier, to say: 'Please teach your grandchildren not to throw litter in the sea.'

I thought about conversation starters, how I could start talking to him to bring it up. He may not even speak enough English. How could I say something without sounding patronising or offensive? In India, you can be sure that it would attract the attention of all the other people on deck.

As we walked from the boat up the hill to the World Heritage Site of Elephanta Caves, we read the signs: 'Keep your Elephanta clean.' There was rubbish everywhere, over on a sad small beach area, down the side of the stalls selling food, drinks and souvenirs, and along the rocks at the side of the jetty. A large cow had its head buried in the bin which it pulled over, leaving contents to spill out.

It is a strange phenomenon when you find yourself surrounded by litter and yet you cannot bring yourself to drop even the tiniest piece. Throughout our time away, I still needed to either carry my rubbish home or wait until I found a bin. I felt guilty using single-use plastic bottles but we had to keep hydrated and more often than not it was the only option.

Elephanta Caves are home to beautiful ancient rock temples, now inhabited by monkeys.

Security guards and members of staff sat lazily in the heat. Near one uniformed officer, I made a point of picking up two large plastic bottles from the ground and I put them in the bin, in front of his nose. Why could he not have done that?

We saw several monkeys carrying plastic bottles, which they steal from tourists. You can't blame them for learning that they can get a nice drink of water. Maybe they are acquiring a taste for Pepsi. One young monkey, scraping around in the rubbish pile, was chewing on a piece of plastic. We reckoned you could teach the monkeys to return the empty bottles to the many rubbish bins before you could teach the ignorant humans.

On returning to Mumbai, docking in front of the landmark Gate of India, we were very aware of the amount of rubbish that accumulated daily in the corner of the harbour. It sits right in front of the prestigious Taj Mahal Palace Hotel, where it costs as much as £800 to stay for one night.

How difficult would it be for the management of that hotel to pay for a cleaner with a net to scoop out all the rubbish? Ten minutes in the morning and ten minutes at night would do it.

Clearly, there are wider issues to be had in terms of educating people not to drop it in the first place, but this would be a good message to start with, to start showing locals and visitors that they care.

Do you know how lucky you are?

'Until one has loved an animal, a part of one's soul remains unawakened'
    —French journalist and novelist Anatole France

When we set off from home on 1 July, Zippy was certainly picking up on the fact that we had carried two large suitcases down the hallway. He ran out of the house, down the front stairs and leapt into the car. It was heartbreaking to turf him out and lock him back in the house. Were we being cruel in going away?

We can only guess what it was like for him when he was running around the streets of Spain, quite possibly scared and lonely. What was it like when he had no shelter from rain or when he was hungry or chased by other dogs or a big truck passed by or it thundered or there were fireworks?

We thought a lot about Zippy when we arrived in Udaipur to be with Animal Aid Unlimited.

I had chosen a homestay on the grounds that the owner, Samvit, had three dogs, two of them St Bernards. Samvit turned out to be the biggest dog lover I have ever met, quite apart from having the biggest dogs I have ever met. He would be the first to admit that dogs, chai and pani puri are his three greatest joys. We all agreed that dogs have only one design fault and that's the length of their lifespan.

Samvit, it turned out, has a heart of gold. Profits from his homestay are put back into the community, invested into a grassroots non-profit organisation providing education to young people in the more rural areas of Udaipur.

At the animal sanctuary we spoke to a fellow volunteer, a woman in her late 50s. 'My room smells of wee,' she moaned, speaking as if she hadn't had a clue that this is what India would be like. 'Yes, the plumbing here leaves a lot to be desired,' we nodded.

'The electricity keeps failing and the wifi is weak and there is the constant noise, dirt in the streets, lunatic drivers, appalling roads, lousy food, so many beggars, everybody has their hand out for a tip, the ATMs don't work, the toilets are disgusting. I hate this place,' she concluded.

Everything she had said was true and yet we love India... and sometimes even we struggle to understand why.

While we spent our days amongst the rescued sick and injured animals at AAU, we realised that many of the staff and volunteers were vegetarian, if not vegan. It wasn't preached at you, but they include a section on animal rights in their Volunteer Manual.

'The cows and donkeys at Animal Aid have opened the eyes of the founders and so many of the volunteers and staff about what happens in the businesses that use animals as commodities — like dairies, poultry farms, or in the leather industry, slaughterhouses and laboratories where animals are used in experimentation,' they say.

'Animals kept in confinement anywhere suffer, and we are continuously reminded of how dearly animals cherish their freedom to roam about. That is why we make every effort to ensure that no animals are tied or confined unless it is essential to their healing or the safety of other animals.

'The animals themselves have lifted our eyes to the sensitivity, the capacity for suffering, the need for joy and play and choices — the need to use their minds as well as their bodies — that all animals possess.

'Not every volunteer at Animal Aid is vegan; some aren't even vegetarian, but we love knowing that every volunteer will have a chance to become closer to all animals, and maybe come to new realisations about the privilege of protecting them, including no longer eating them or using them for their products.'

They also gave the following advice about animal welfare in India:

'Snake charmers: Cobras in a basket are always kept in that basket until they die about a month or so later after their venom glands have been burned or cut out. Their salivary glands are injured in this barbaric process and they cannot survive. Forced to live curled up in a tiny basket and only taken on to be surrounded by crowds and taunted is the cruellest abuse and must not be entertained. It is also illegal under the Wildlife Protection Act.

'Camel or other bone: You might be told that there is bone inlaid in a table top that has come from a camel or other animal who died a natural death. This is not true. Every time you purchase an animal product you are sponsoring an animal's death.

'Milk: India is one of the world's largest producers of milk. If you are drinking milk in India because you believe cows are treated better here, it is not the case. Every glass of milk tea or lassi is the milk that belonged to a mother's baby and is being starved and tied, killed or abandoned on the road.

'Eggs: 80% of eggs in India were laid by hens confined in factory farm battery cages. These hens will live their whole lives, about two years, in hellacious confinement until they are slaughtered. Chickens are every bit as maternal as other animals but are robbed of their every mothering need to nest and care for their babies.'

Zippy is the true start of our vegan journey (him, and a wingless bee).

Our Spanish furball arrived on 26 January 2015. Adorable from the minute he walked in to our lives, tail wagging, we knew he fitted in. It was as if he knew this was his forever home.

He hasn't put a paw wrong since, if we don't count the time he cocked his leg against my daughter's photo on the hearth, which was our fault really as we had friends around and we failed to spot that he was crossing his legs.

Zippy is half Spanish water dog, though we are not sure which half. He doesn't speak Spanish and he doesn't like water, not the sea, anyway. He doesn't swim but will enjoy playing with stones and seaweed in flat-calm rock pools.

In recent years people have come to talk of their happy place. I know exactly where mine is (apart from Udaipur). It's our beach at low tide, 'our' beach being the one just a five-minute walk from our front door. It is possibly the least touristy beach of Jersey and I love it all the more for that. Jersey has one of the largest tidal ranges in the world, more than 12 m on spring tides. Not only does it clean our beaches, it also creates some beautiful landscapes on a daily basis.

On the south-east coast the tide can recede 3.2 km, revealing one of the most amazing spaces, a designated Wetland of International Importance under the Ramsar Convention of 2000, a place where we have been enchanted by night-time walks to see tiny glowing worms in the sand, which display what is known as bioluminescence.

Our beach changes with the time of day, the state of the tide, the wind and the rain. It's particularly sublime when the sea is flat calm and the tide is just turning to come back in. The ripples in the sand, the worm casts, the shells, the rock pools with crabs and tiny fish darting about, the egrets, the dogs enjoying their daily walk. Sometimes I sit on a rock and just sit and stare out to sea. Zippy will sit patiently nearby.

We often ask him if he knows how lucky he is. I think he does. Zippy had been living the bachelor life on the streets of Cartagena, evading capture for six months. He would have been taken to the kill station if no home had been found for him. An animal rescue charity cleaned him up, shaved off his matted and flea-ridden coat, vaccinated, micro-chipped and castrated him. The full monty. They put him in a van with several other lucky dogs to make the long journey through Spain and France, north to St Malo and the one-hour ferry across to Jersey.

For a dog with a challenged past, Zippy seemed remark-ably relaxed when he arrived and keen to make a good impression. As he ambled towards me on the first day, I said that we would not allow him to get on the sofa. He jumped up. Ok, I said, but not our bed. Definitely not our bed.

That first night he slept in my daughter's room, on her bed, tucked under her arm, his head very nearly on her pillow. For a few nights, he slept in his basket at the side of our bed. And then, one morning, he was so excited to see us that he ran around and jumped on the bed. We hesitated a split second too long, he claimed victory and he never looked back. We soon learned how a dog can double in size when stretching out on a duvet.

He even behaved himself when he was allowed to stay with us at a five-star hotel, although he got up on the bed there too. If his friends could see him now.

As we got to know Zippy we fell hopelessly in love with him. We will never know his complete history but, from his behaviour and nature, we don't think he was ever hurt, and we suspect that he was once loved or at least cared for. Perhaps he was lost or abandoned. I particularly love Zippy's smell and I can't help kissing him on the top of his head several times a day, mostly in the morning and again at night.

We didn't hear Zippy's bark for at least three months. Even now, he only occasionally comes out with a single woof when he whips himself into a frenzy of pre-walk excitement, and he always looks as surprised as we are.

David's view is that Zippy is nicer than any person he knows. (Er, thanks.) What he likes is that he is non-judgmental and loves unconditionally. 'He is just kind and gentle,' he tells me, a tear in his eye. David is most definitely the soppier of the two of us. On pretty much a daily basis, I laugh at his ability to well up at the smallest of things. Barnado's TV adverts. Opera. Heck, once he even cried at a dessert that was put in front of him at a particularly nice restaurant.

The thought of life without Zippy fills him with dread. Someone once said that dogs have shorter life spans than we do because they have less to learn. We are reminded of the cartoon of two dogs sitting at the gates of heaven. A very old bearded man tells the dogs: 'You do know you're welcome to come in, don't you?' and one of the two dogs replies: 'It's okay, we're waiting for someone.'

And David is crying again.

Zippy is the kind of dog who makes passing strangers smile. He is almost cartoon-like in his perfection, with his black 'mask' on his eyes, one ear white, the other black.

We love him so totally that it is difficult to describe if you haven't known the love of a dog. It's completely different to cats. Our household has traditionally favoured feline over canine... Lester, Gazza, Tinker, Elmo. Elmo, a gentle tabby, lived to the amazing age of 19. When Zippy arrived, Elmo was about 17 and she had never lived with a dog before. On being introduced, Zippy made like he was invisible and withdrew into a corner, trying to make himself half his size and looking the other way to demonstrate his submission. Elmo treated him with indifference and after a little bit of hissing, they got along ok.

We weren't going to get another cat after Elmo was peacefully put to sleep, but we inherited Scooby, a gentle ginger mog, whose back end is a tad wobbly ever since a car accident. He can be remarkably clumsy for a cat, which amuses us no end.

Because Zippy is such a pacifist, they get on just fine.

David blames his journey towards veganism not just on Zippy, but also on a bee. On Facebook there was the story of a woman who found a bee in her garden and she wondered why it made no attempt to fly away. On closer examination she noticed that the bee, though fully grown, had no wings.

Noticing how inactive it was, she dissolved some sugar in water and offered the bee the energy drink. Over the next five months the bee lived happily in a small but comfortable environment the woman had created for him. The bee would climb up the woman's finger and crawl along her arm quite happily. One night, the bee went to sleep one final time.

It struck David how the bee, a simple creature, an earthling, had as much right to live as we do.

Towards the end of our Asian adventure, we considered getting another rescue dog. His name was Marvin, a galgo, an ancient breed of Spanish greyhound, the most persecuted dog in Spain. I had never heard of it before.

I read on www.thedodo.com: 'The galgos are greyhounds used for hunting, but most are used for only one season and then discarded. If they hunt poorly, they are tortured as retribution for the shame they reflected upon their owners.

'The reasoning of the galgueros is that by torturing and killing the dogs they wash away the dishonour the dogs displayed that brought shame to their masters. In reality, the practice is simply an exercise in sadism that involves burning the dogs with acid, dragging them behind cars, sacrificing them to fighting dogs, skinning them alive or burying them alive. The most famous torture is called the piano dance, this involves hanging the dog by the neck with the feet just touching the ground as it struggles to breathe and slowly is strangled to death by its movements.'

I mean, seriously? In a western, so-called developed country, in 2019, this practice goes on? I felt sick to my stomach. Under Spanish law they are classified as working dogs and therefore not protected the way that pets would be.

And the worst thing? Every year, about 50,000 galgos die in this barbaric way.

50,000.

For fuck's sake.

This level of cruelty really messes with my head. Round up some galgueros and do the same to them in public, that's what I say. What will it take to stop it?

I see the same helplessness and utter incredulity in comedian and actor Ricky Gervais' face when he speaks of the Yulin Meat Festival in China. There are clips of him on YouTube describing it as the most horrendous thing he's ever heard of. It's a horrific practice where people torture dogs, blow-torching, beating, boiling, skinning them — all while they are still alive. All this because they believe that the adrenaline caused by the fear and pain makes the meat taste better.

In true Gervais fashion, he doesn't hold back in describing the perpetrators as fucking mental sadistic c***s. Sorry if the swearing offends, but please be more offended by the abuse. It's hell, he says. Be offended.

Good on you, Ricky. Let's not couch it softly. Let's not look away. Let's not pretend it doesn't happen.

I'd go further. Skin the perpetrators alive. See how they like it.

Bastards.

It distresses me that people can be so cruel to animals in so many different ways. In Nepal, every five years in a village called Bariyapur, there is a festival celebrating the goddess

Gadhimai. In 2009 the sacrifice reached new heights, with a quarter of a million animals killed.

If only someone would tell them it was all made up in some bloke's mind hundreds of years ago. If only someone would sway it the other way and say that such animal sacrifice will bring the wrath of their god (or goddess) upon them.

I just hope that people power can and will achieve change. After international outrage, PETA (People for the Ethical Treatment of Animals) reported that this happened in time for 2019: 'The Gadhimai Temple Trust hereby declares our formal decision to end animal sacrifice. With your help, we can ensure Gadhimai 2019 is free from bloodshed. Moreover, we can ensure Gadhimai 2019 is a momentous celebration of life.'

I am crossing my fingers that there is hope after all.

The life of a street dog in India is, of course, very different to the life of a pet dog in Jersey. I suppose if you took the vegan argument to the extreme, you could argue that our pet dogs are in captivity and that it is the street dog who has his freedom. But he doesn't necessarily have easy access to decent food and clean water. Or a vet. Apart from the hazard of traffic, he can enjoy a reasonably happy life, fathering puppies, having his own pack around him, and lazing in the sun.

There are millions of street dogs in India, around 10,000 in Udaipur alone. We learned that Animal Aid Unlimited work hard to return dogs to the same place that they were picked up — they are, after all, street dogs who most likely have packs to return to. So long as they are strong enough to fend for themselves and find food, they can be released.

AAU rightly say that to try to rehome them all would be impossible and not a wise use of their resources. The majority of street dogs are doing very well. They are well adapted to the street, they were born there, and likely live with their parents, siblings or pups. Most dogs who come into the sanctuary are out again after a month.

Having spent a couple of weeks with Animal Aid, we knew that street dogs in India are largely happy in the communities where they live. They scavenge for food but some people look out for those nearby their homes and shops. But many people are wary of them, and not just wary but scared, which will lead them to shoo them away aggressively.

All through India, I never did get used to hearing dogs barking at night, as they defended their territory or saw off a nasty human. And it was distressing to see how close they lived to busy roads. Every day you would see dogs trying to find a path through the traffic. Some didn't make it.

On 31 October, Halloween, after 18 days in Udaipur, I shared a post on Facebook. I wrote: 'Animal rights is now the biggest social justice issue since the abolition of slavery. I make no excuse for starting to share posts like these. If you like scary movies, then watch Dominion, Land of Hope and Glory or Earthlings.'

The post I shared was one from Earthling Ed, who said: 'For non-human animals, life on this planet is worse than the narrative of the scariest horror movie you could ever imagine. They are enslaved, they are beaten, they are mutilated, they are torn away from their friends and families, they are castrated, they have their teeth pulled out, they have their skin ripped from their bodies, they are maimed, they are tortured, they are boiled alive, they are cut into pieces and they are eaten.

'The constant state of terror that billions and billions of individuals are living in right now is completely unfathomable. We can never understand the level of pain, the level of fear and the level of utter frantic confusion and panic that they live in. We can try to articulate it in words but we can never express the magnitude of their suffering.'

Sawubona — 'I see you'

'We make a living by what we get,
But we make a life by what we give'
—*Winston Churchill*

In India we saw a beggar who was prostrate, limbs gangly in all directions, as if he had landed splat on the ground like the coyote from the Road Runner cartoon. He inched forward, pushing an aluminium pot in front of him to collect money, pulling himself forward with his arms. It raised so many questions.

Where is he from? How does he live his life? Where does he live and with whom? Was he born like this? Has he been deliberately crippled? Who put him on the street? Does he get picked up (literally) at the end of the day? Is he exploited by anyone? How does he eat? How does he go to the toilet? How much money does he make in a day? Is it enough? Has he ever been hit by a car? Where is the health and social security system of this country? What does it say about a country that allows this to happen? How does he feel?

What is his name?

Try walking a mile in his shoes. If indeed he could walk. Or had shoes.

Sometimes you have got to open your eyes to the things going on in the world.

We were aware that children are often maimed so that they can be pimped out as beggars on the streets. The film Slumdog Millionaire depicted this with a scene that I can hardly bring myself to watch. Jamal's friend, a young boy in the home where they are living, has a burning hot liquid poured in his eyes to blind him. It happens.

I used to score beggars out of ten. It was just something I and my fellow travellers did when on my first visit to India, when I was 19. If there was little wrong with them, they might merit only 1 or 2. As we went through India, then and now, we realised that there are some who score 10 out of 10.

Initially David thought this was a little heartless. He is more likely to want to give the beggar something. In Paris, in the year we got married, we saw a man, possibly Rwandan, who had no arms or legs perched on a street near Notre Dame with a begging bowl. It was clear that this was no birth defect. He had significant scarring. Both the para-medic in David and the journalist in me wanted to know his story but we walked on by, as you do. We did, however, quickly agree that he was easily a 10. Too flippant? Were we just having a joke, a coping mechanism, knowing we could do nothing about it?

One time, we visited New York, where a man approached us for money and David simply got his wallet out and started sifting through his notes before handing one or two over. I was mortified. I mean, that man could have snatched the wallet and run, or he may have a gang watching him, or... or... Instead, what happened was the man was extremely grateful and walked away. Another lesson for me, perhaps.

On a previous trip to Nepal, David went up to one or two street lepers to speak to them and give them some cash. It always attracted a few looks from locals. David's attitude has always been that if you give to those worse off than yourself you should do so with a good heart and no agenda, and he realised that he felt better if he donated without any request even for a photograph. He is ok with the fact that often his good nature might be abused by those who make a good living by pleading poverty but he says it's balanced by the fact that sometimes a small donation really does make a big difference to those who are genuinely in need. And he believes in karma.

The cow which had a fifth leg coming out of its neck came as a surprise. Of course, with the cow being sacred, an animal like this is considered special. Touch the leg and you'll get good luck. More likely it will bring good luck to the owner who wants to make a few rupees. Good luck to him. If he's being entrepreneurial and if it means the animal is actually well looked after, fed and watered, then fair enough.

It was quite bizarre when we saw it the first time. And even more bizarre when a modern and wealthier Indian man came up to move the leg around to see if it was fake. That hadn't even crossed my mind until then. It was real all right. I was just glad to see that the decorated cow was not in any pain or distress. And we were to see another later on in our journey, by which time we were blasé about it and we just thought, oh look, there's another mutant cow.

Up until now, we had been surprised by how laid-back Indian drivers appeared to be. Yes, traffic was crazy, drivers were always hooting and they didn't follow rules of the road but we never saw road rage and at least they all seemed to follow a system, which basically boiled down to this: Give way to anything bigger than yourself. So that works for buses, lorries, cars, tuk-tuks, motorbikes, bicycles, pedestrians. They know their pecking order. Unless you're an animal. Water buffalo, cows and dogs wander as they wish, sitting where they like, sleeping in the middle of the road.

Mainly, the driving we had seen was on slow roads. Traffic could not go too fast because of the potholes, construction work, rubble and, of course, other traffic. But on the road from Udaipur to Jodhpur, we spent some of the time on a two-lane highway where slow lorries hogged the outside lane. One minute our driver was overtaking on the left, then on the right, and occasionally there would be a barricade in the road with incredibly little warning, either put there by police to slow the traffic or put there to allow roadworks (where there were always women in saris carrying concrete on their heads). The equivalent roadworks in the UK would have about a mile of warning cones. Here, you were lucky if there were three cones before the hazard appeared.

Right in front of us, two large lorries found themselves side by side at the same speed. One wouldn't give way to the other. They got scarily close to the point that I gasped, thinking it was accidental. And then I realised they were doing it on purpose. One of the drivers was deliberately trying to force the other off the road. The other retaliated and pushed back. Then a third lorry somehow came up and got involved and stopped, causing us to put on the brakes, and the driver jumped out brandishing a sturdy stick. At which point our driver pulled around to the left on the stony hard shoulder and we carried on our journey, safely out of the way. It was clear that he didn't think it would be a good idea to stop to interfere.

On another occasion, we needed to get to a restaurant on the other side of the two-lane highway. Our driver crossed over in a gap in the central reservation and proceeded to drive on what was the hard shoulder – in the opposite direction to the oncoming traffic. No one batted an eyelid. They didn't even hoot.

Indians like hooting. It's their favourite pastime. It's even painted on the back of most vehicles. 'Horn OK.' 'Horn please.' But Indians are surely oblivious to the sound. It all becomes white noise. One driver we knew hooted at every corner, even when he had not looked the other way. It was as if he thought that a hoot meant he could proceed.

Tuk-tuk drivers passed vehicles and pedestrians with inches to spare. They didn't stop if they saw something coming. They might have slowed down but they otherwise just kept going until people squeezed past and somehow, if everyone breathed in, they managed it. On the roads, I enjoyed the signs we passed, misspellings everywhere… Dormetri, Resturent, Biffe (buffet) and Neight College, signs for places like Cumbum, Hotel Decent and Terminal Cum Pumping Station, and a town called Dudu.

One young man had three children under five on his motorbike. We passed a few lorries and tractors which were so laden with hay that they just looked like super-sized haystacks on wheels. Despite the evident basic way of life in the villages we passed through, the children always looked so smart in their brown and beige uniforms and everywhere there were red signs for 'Airtel 4G, the smartphone network'. They stood out because they were not yet faded or covered in dust. And, we observed, mobile phone technology has beaten basic plumbing to the most rural areas.

On reaching Jodhpur, we had the best tuk-tuk drive into the town. It was busy at 5 pm and everyone was hooting. Our young driver, who most likely had not been to tuk-tuk driving school, was for a while on his mobile phone. I was about to have a word when I realised he was putting Indian music on his speakers. The music just made us grin, as we whizzed in through the crowded Sardar Market past the Clock Tower and into the alleyways of the old city.

During the day, the market is alive with people selling all kinds of things, from Diwali stickers and firecrackers to brightly coloured scarves and sandals. The area around the Clock Tower is touristy but initial prices are probably ten times what vendors will settle for.

But where there are white faces, there are inevitably beggars. Many scruffy children approached us, often tugging on our clothes to draw attention to themselves.

They indicated that they were hungry.

One morning, three girls came up to us. Admittedly, they did look like they could do with a decent meal. Instead of giving them a handful of coins, we gave in to their requests for food. We took them to a roadside stall and ordered them an omelette each. It cost more than giving them each a coin, but it was a far more satisfactory outcome all round.

We found ourselves making judgment calls each time we saw a beggar. Some we ignored, others we acknowledged. Some were grateful, others less so. One woman we gave to berated us for not giving enough. One young girl didn't want to accept a note because it was slightly torn. Another, who followed us for way too long, wanted more than the few small coins we gave her. Cheeky beggars. You do sometimes have to ignore them and we didn't give them the time of day when an area was crowded. If you give to one child, you'll find that 20 more suddenly come out of the woodwork. You also don't want to be getting money out, exposing where you keep your wallet and making yourself vulnerable to a thief.

It had become a bit of a routine each morning, sorting out 10- and 20-rupee notes and other coins. We also took biscuits and cakes from our generous breakfast, ready to hand out to grateful hungry children. We never had to carry them for very long.

Actually, since Udaipur, we gave biscuits to dogs, banana skins to cows, and shampoo sachets and pens to children.

A couple of days later, our sarcasm reached new heights when beggar children were in our face before we had even got out of a tuk-tuk. We had arrived at a temple and a couple of scruffy children had their hands out, demanding 'money' and 'chocolate'. It must be the first words they learn.

No, sorry, it's not your day, we said. Go to school. Get a good job. We talked and talked at them and continued to say no. They were persistent and irritating and we told them so.

Another day, one young girl came up to our tuk-tuk in very heavy traffic and asked for money. She was unaccompanied. She had a sad little face. She was no more than five years old.

It was funny. Many people in Jodhpur seemed to have the same hobby. One day, we were walking and talking to some boys who had tagged along. They were practising their English.

'What's your hobby?' they asked. So we mentioned photography, pointing to the whopping great clue around David's neck.

'What's yours?' we asked. 'Football? Cricket?'

No, it turned out to be collecting foreign bank-notes. Of course! We didn't have anything to give them and probably wouldn't have put our hands in our pockets in this instance anyway.

Earlier the same day, as we were walking up a tiny back street to the fort, we said 'namaste' to an older man standing in his doorway. 'Where are you from?' was the question we were asked more than any other.

'England,' we said. Ah, England, his favourite. We knew it would be. 'Very, very good.'

He started talking about his sons and how one of them loved history. And oh look, within arm's reach by the front door, was his foreign bank-note collection in a small photo album. David wanted to return the next day with an English £10 note, but the cynic in me said it was begging by any other name. We had, after all, been advised by our haveli owners to be wary of people chatting to us. They tended to be over-friendly and would say they were best friends or brothers with the haveli owner in order to gain your trust somehow.

Later, at the end of our adventure, we would join a walking tour of Old Delhi. It just so happened that our guide was delayed and we had to wait for an hour outside the Jama Masjid, a mosque and popular tourist spot. We chatted amiably to the gentleman selling small wicker baskets from which a plastic cobra popped up. We watched the beggar children. One minute they were running around playing with each other. The next, they would stand at the gates of the mosque, looking forlorn and putting their hands to their mouths. A coach-load of Chinese tourists had arrived.

We observed how all these visitors ignored the beggars and the vendors trying to sell water, jewellery or small fake snakes in a wicker pot. Four years ago we were those tourists. After three months in a country, however, you see it differently. We would at least smile or acknowledge the beggars.

In Rajasthan, there had been a man who was sitting outside a large temple. We were conscious that we were about to talk to the street cow and a couple of friendly dogs over the road. And yet we would be ignoring a human being who had severely deformed legs. David approached him, smiled and gave him a note which was probably a lot more than what that beggar earned in a day, but to us was little more than the cost of a cappuccino. His face lit up with a smile and he put his hands together in a genuine gesture of gratitude. He kissed the money and said thank you by touching his heart.

Asked for a piece of life advice, former US president Bill Clinton* said: 'I've come to believe that one of the most important things is to see people. The person who opens the door for you, the person who pours your coffee. Acknowledge them. Show them respect. The traditional greeting of the Zulu people of South Africa is Sawubona. It means "I see you". I try and do that.'

I like to think that we saw the beggars.

*And that's the same Bill Clinton who went vegan in 2010 after emergency heart surgery.

Having adopted a healthier lifestyle, he said: 'All my blood tests are good, and my vital signs are good, and I feel good, and I also have, believe it or not, more energy.'

Diwali in the desert

'The more helpless the creature, the more that it is entitled to protection by man from the cruelty of man'

—*Mahatma Gandhi*

Sometimes I fucking hate India.

It was November, and we were heading towards Diwali, the festival of light. If ever I came across a copy of the Times of India, I would enjoy flicking through it. Sometimes I wish I hadn't.

In one article, I read that owls were being trapped up in the hills of Uttarakhand. These were the bullet points under the headline 'Brutal Practice':

*India has 30 owl species, mostly threatened or endangered.

*Owl sacrifice during Diwali is believed to bring prosperity.

*The price for a bird ranges from Rs 300 to Rs 50,000 for larger species. [approx £3 — £540]

*Rock eagle owl, dusky eagle owl and brown fish owl are most preferred.

*Tantrik rituals during Diwali involve blinding, dismembering or burying owls alive.

How is this even possible? We are not living in the bloody Dark Ages. This made me both angry and sad for weeks. The appalling cruelty is so totally unnecessary.

Why can't a great Indian leader change people's views by telling them that harming owls will do the very opposite of bringing prosperity? Instead, they should all be told that it will bring shame on them and their family. It's all made up in someone's head as it is.

Although Diwali is the festival of light, really it has become the festival of noise, which, for India, is saying something. All around our haveli in Jaisalmer we had non-stop firecrackers and fireworks. Some were so loud it was like a bomb had gone off. So it was nice that we were spending the main day of Diwali (like our Christmas Day) in the Thar desert. We were joined by two other couples, sitting on simple beds around a camp fire as the sun went down.

Our two guides whipped up a thali, complete with rice and chapatis, and served them with a chilled beer. Then they produced fireworks and sparklers. We all had a bit of child-like fun making shapes with our sparklers. Although we created a little noise it was brief and we returned to our peace. The air was still, everyone settled back into a thoughtful silence as we stared at the flames from the fire or the carpet of stars above us, which seemed to get closer and brighter with every passing hour.

Our beds for the night were open to the elements. At least we were raised off the ground, away from the large black beetles that were patrolling the sand. I didn't mind them being there but I didn't fancy sharing my boudoir with them. At the best of times, I find it difficult to sleep in a new bed in a new hotel, so it wasn't surprising that I was not going to sleep well on a basic bed frame, with incredibly heavy layers of blankets. We needed them too as the temperature dropped to 16 degrees — easily half the daytime temperature. Because of the contrast, it felt colder still. Strangely, I didn't mind my fitful sleep. It was magical to open my eyes to the view of the night-time stars, with no light or noise pollution. One time I turned over, glanced up and saw a shooting star.

In the morning, it was wise to get up early to hide behind a bush to go to the toilet before anyone else was walking around camp. As it got just a little bit lighter, we could hear Samboo calling: 'Chai, chai.' We grabbed a cup and clambered to the top of a dune to wait for the sun to rise. It was beautiful, sending new colours across the landscape and creating dramatic shadows from the ridges on the dunes. The only sound was of bells on sheep and goats in the distance.

While we waited, our guides cooked up a good breakfast and all too soon we were on our way back to our haveli — but not before we met some camels. A small group of tourists were riding them back to the village. We later spoke to one couple staying at our haveli who told us they had been assured beforehand that the camels were well looked after and they verified that appeared to be the case. They explained that the camels had been allowed to wander off at night, albeit with certain restrictions. They had been hobbled with a small bit of rope around their front legs, preventing them from walking further than 3 or 4 km. So in the morning the guides had to round them all up, causing their group some amusement as they waited.

As we were on a journey towards veganism, the ethics of camel-riding had been taking up quite a lot of our mealtime conversations. Everyone we had spoken to had been ok with it. Online, we couldn't find any clear controversy that said it should be avoided at all costs. Indeed, on TripAdvisor, camel-riding still consistently gets five stars on outdoor activities in Jaisalmer. The conclusion would seem to be summed up by this: Choose your tour company carefully. Camels should be in good condition, properly fed, watered and rested, though I am not sure how exactly you can ensure this before you book. You can ask the right questions but I suspect most tour agencies will give you the answer you wish to hear.

Camels, the ships of the desert, have been domesticated for 2,000 years. *That doesn't mean it's right,* I hear someone argue. For hundreds of years they have been used to transport goods across the desert. *But we have cars and lorries to do that now.* These are relatively poor people, who cannot afford vehicles — or the vehicles can't go where the camels can. *Ok, that's the reasoning for using camels in their 'day job'. Why should a tourist ride a camel, when they can ride in a jeep as an alternative?*

What are the ethics of a tourist riding a camel? Is it any different to riding a horse — with the caveats that the animals in all cases should have proper care, food, water, shelter and rest? There will be some who argue that you should not ride any animal for human pleasure, sport or entertainment full-stop. Horses have to go through a breaking and training process, just like camels do.

We were able to get close enough to camels to take photos. We could not miss the fact that they had chunky pegs through their noses so that their owner could control them, getting them to follow on a rope or getting them to sit and stand. Ideally, pegs would be put in under anaesthetic and with due veterinary care. I am pretty sure that wouldn't have been the case here.

While the camels were being saddled up, there were many layers of covers and cushions put on and straps under their belly. So far so good. It was when the saddle was put on, which was pretty heavy in its own right, that the camel grunted and grumbled. Although I am no expert on camel communication, I concluded that it was a bit irritated by it.

As we discovered, it's all very well trying to do your research on the spot by asking the drivers questions, but their English is limited. You can't get a full conversation with them, though it is clear that this is their livelihood and it makes a lot of sense for them to care for their camels. We saved ourselves the discomfort (mental and physical) and hopped back in the jeep for the fast, bumpy, sandy, sweaty ride back to the haveli.

Most of the poorest communities we met during our travels have a relationship with animals quite unlike we do. In Vietnam and Cambodia, with their long history of war, poverty and near-starvation, people have until recently been obliged to eat whatever they could get their hands on, including cats and dogs. But although we love our pets, we have no problem killing and eating equally sentient pigs, sheep and cows. The scale of intensive farming to satisfy our lust for meat has led to the most barbaric crime against billions of animals.

And yet we continued to wonder whether we were in any position to judge those who don't enjoy the choices that we have. Putting aside any large-scale industries for a moment, many people in Asia breed livestock to feed their families. Unlike us, many of them can't pop down to Waitrose to buy organic, ethically sourced vegan ready-meals. We have to remind ourselves that we judge from a very privileged position.

The indigenous people who live in the villages on the edges of the Thar Desert are some of the poorest people in a poor country. In this harsh climate their lives are a constant battle for survival. Some make enough to feed their families by facilitating camel rides. The villagers we met seemed to take good care of their animals which are essential to their livelihood and very existence.

Certainly tourists will have fed much of the cruelty to animals, albeit unwittingly, and now it is the more enlightened generation of tourists who must vote with their feet and via social media to bring an end to some appalling abuses: dancing bears, caged and drugged wild cats, whales in fish tanks and elephants who have witnessed the cold-blooded murder of their mothers to then suffer the physical and emotional abuse known as Phajaan.

Maybe camels and camel-riding will be the next thing that tourists will have to think twice about.

We had never even heard of Pushkar or its famous annual Camel Fair when we left home. It turned out that when we reached the town, it was only days away and preparations had begun. Herders had started arriving with their camels and plenty of traders had already laid out their stalls. There was every bit of equipment and adornment you could ever need for camel-keeping.

Each year, around 200,000 people converge on this small town, right near our guest house, as it happened, and they bring some 50,000 camels, horses and cattle. There is serious business to be done, before it becomes a strange mix of side-shows, including snake charmers, children balancing on poles and 'visitors versus locals' wrestling matches.

We took a walk around the dusty showground, fairground and camel-parking area, four days ahead of the start of the event. It was not a pretty sight. I didn't like it one little bit.

It distressed me to see two horses tied up in a tent, where a man was swinging a heavy hammer to knock in some more tent pegs. The horses were clearly terrified by the noise and could merely shy away, as far as their two metres of rope would allow. The man was oblivious.

I would have expected that if you were here to sell, your camels would be healthy specimens. But they weren't. The ones pulling heavy carts laden with humans were not in the best condition. On the face of it, the ones taking tourists for rides on their backs seemed to be better cared for. But it was the area at the back where people had parked their camels that saddened me. Some had been painted and decorated. One was having a peg inserted into its nose and it was clearly unhappy about it. We watched a child no older than eight needlessly thwacking a camel with a stick. Another was being walked and a different child started picking up stones and throwing them at its back legs. Again, absolutely no reason. The camel was walking with no fuss, being led on a harness and rope. I said 'no' to the boy twice. He did it again and looked back. I shook my head. He stuck his tongue out and backed off.

We are not going to change a culture that has had this kind of fair for hundreds of years. But what I came away wishing more than anything was that someone would please provide more education about animal welfare. They can keep camels, horses and cows for their livelihood but for God's sake (whichever one you want to believe in) be nice to them.

Is there no organisation in India that could set up several stalls at the camel fair and spread the word about why it is good to be kind to your animals? Ahimsa. Speak in their language, speak in a way their culture and religion will understand. It surely must be possible.

Photography is prohibited on the ghats that surround the holy lake of Pushkar. The first time that we attempted to have a walk around the lake, a man yelled at David simply for having a large camera around his neck, even though he wasn't taking photos. It's difficult to argue with someone who is so angry at you for something you haven't actually done.

What they really mean is, don't take pictures of people bathing at the ghats. Fair enough. After all, it's a sacred site. A dip here is believed to cleanse sins and cure skin diseases. Hindus try to make a pilgrimage here at least once in their life, and large numbers come especially around the Kartik Purnima festival in October/November.

But plenty of people, Indians included, continue to use their mobile phones to take selfies all the time, even in the busiest areas, and it seemed to me that the man should have been directing his energy at them. And the busiest areas might involve men stripped down to their pants or women who keep half a sari around their waist, but expose their top half. This tended to be old women, but it seemed to be in contradiction with how they can tut-tut if you as a white woman so much as bare your shoulders.

Around the lake, you have to take off your shoes and, as we were going to walk all around it, we decided to carry ours with us. At one point we sat to enjoy the view (of the lake, not the topless women), and David put his shoes on the floor. Horror of horrors, it turned out that it was just within what is considered to be the sacred bit.

Three men in matching T-shirts marched up to us. They picked up David's shoes and were about to put them in their large bin. Luckily we swiftly retaliated, apologising, and got them back. The men moved on to where an elderly lady was sitting. They yanked the flip-flops from her feet, threw them into their sin bin, shouting and making a fuss. I couldn't believe how rude they were, particularly to an older lady who had clearly meant no harm.

As someone who celebrates the beauty of all people, young, old, male, female, beautifully formed or cruelly deformed, David kept muttering something about India being God's gift to photographers. He prefers taking pictures of people and street life to temples and landscapes (though he enjoys those too). But it brought with it a daily dilemma, even when he was equipped with a decent zoom lens.

'Indian people have an indefinable beauty,' he says. 'Indian people wear colourful clothes, women in their amazing saris and kurtis, a huge melting pot of joyous beauty, set against the poor, the dirty and the deformed.

'As we became more aware of the negative impact of tourism, and watched others on our travels, we couldn't help but feel uncomfortable that when we indiscriminately photo-graphed the people we met, we were turning the foreign places we visited into some kind of human spectacle.'

We saw one young Indian man blatantly put his phone up in an old lady's face to get a photo. We had both seen the shot, knew it would make a great photo, but felt there was no way of taking it without invading her privacy, which is exactly what that man did. And after that we certainly couldn't do it. We said 'namaste' politely and moved on.

How would we feel if, when we were back home going about our normal daily life, a tourist just took photos of us, particularly without asking or even attempting to talk to us?

Some people we met would ask us to take their photo and were just as keen to get endless selfies with us. Others made it clear they did not wish to be digitally immortalised on some stranger's Facebook feed.

When does education and reportage become voyeurism? At the end of each day, subject to a reasonable wifi connection, David enjoyed sharing his favourite images on Facebook, but found himself questioning his motives. Was it just a way of letting family know we were safe? Was it to say, hey, look what amazing thing (good, bad or funny) we have seen today? Was it to wind up friends who were sitting at their office desks? Or was it simply that he was enjoying his hobby, creating a piece of art, capturing a moment in time?

The Holy Men were in town for the camel fair and accompanying religious festival. Some were genuine, many were not, and I couldn't tell the difference. You could identify them easily enough, with their orange clothes, sticks, painted faces, long grey hair and long beards.

We had dinner at a restaurant which had a view down on to the road and we watched as a number of men sat on the temple steps, accepting donations from worshippers. The waiter told us they were babas, people who had no family. They issued blessings in return for a few rupees. We had a nice moussaka as monkeys passed by on the window sills.

As we walked the circumference of the lake, we stopped to talk to a baba in the shade of a tree. We declined his offer of tea. David gave him his travel towel, which he had been wanting to get rid of anyway. There was no word of a thank-you. The baba seemed more interested in asking for money for vegetables to make dinner. The annoying thing was not knowing which were real, whether they were a sadhu or a saddo, a fakir or a faker.

From Pushkar, we posted another parcel home. While we waited for our parcel to be sewn up in muslin, we sat on a step opposite enjoying watching daily life unfold in this small non-touristy side street. The young man next door was preparing his shop for business. He had lively chanting music which he would occasionally happily join in with. As everyone in India seems to do, he was using a small brush to sweep away the rubbish from outside his shop, leaving it either in his neighbour's territory to the side, further in to the middle of the street, or into the drainage channel at the kerb-side. He whipped his display cabinet to get the dust off and used newspaper and water to clean the glass frontage. Then he threw the newspaper into the road.

The sewing man paused to have a chai from a small paper cup, which he casually threw into the street afterwards. This is just what happens, but it never failed to astonish us.

The water delivery man arrived in a battered old van. He put one blue barrel on someone's doorstep and removed the empty one. Cows passed by, mingling with motorbikes and pedestrians. A man came and stood next to us. He brought up a load of sputum, a great guttural sound, and spat on the street right next to me.

Once our parcel was sewn up, the man offered to take us to the nearest post office. Why not, we thought. So we hopped on his motorbike, all three of us, parcel balanced on the handlebars, not a helmet in sight, David holding on at the back for all he was worth. Any of the bumps or potholes could have sent him flying or, more worryingly, the parcel. At the post office, they lacked pens, marker pens, duct tape and queuing systems, and they seemed to have run out of courtesy too. Two young women pushed in, resulting in some choice sarcasm from us. I was sure they understood English — most Indian women their age do. Once we had completed our transaction, we thanked the post office worker behind the counter. He didn't look up. He didn't say a word. He just continued to look down at some paperwork and with that we walked away, David muttering: 'Pleasure doing business with you.'

It was amusing observing other foreigners. It was easy to spot those who considered themselves travellers, rather than tourists. Many would not acknowledge us, as they would pass us with the air of 'I'm cool, I've been here longer than you, I'm not just a tourist'.

You could spot them in their baggy trousers, vest tops, long hair tied up, and that was just the men. The men would always have a beard and sometimes a little scarf around their neck. Girls would likely have nose piercings and tattoos. And they would all have a certain swagger, a laid-back lollop. But then I noticed that we were morphing into those people. We had a smugness from being on the road for six months, especially when we saw white people getting off coaches, being ferried straight to the sightseeing point, ignoring all the vibrancy of the street because they were too scared to stop and look and interact.

I was in loose baggy trousers simply because they were cool (as in temperature) and practical. My bare white middle-aged legs weren't going to offend anyone, temple or not. The laid-back lollop develops from the need to conserve energy in the heat as well as the wonderful realisation that, actually, you are not in a hurry like you are back home with a full-time job and kids to run around after.

We loved the internationality of travelling, meeting people from Mexico, Israel, Australia, Spain, Germany. Talking to interesting and articulate young people made us feel young again and I think we got a bit of respect when they realised that we too were longer-term travellers.

Before he decided to let his beard grow in the last few weeks, David had a fascination for street barbers. After each trim, he couldn't wait for his hair to grow again so he could find another. At one stop in Rajasthan, he couldn't find a street barber and had to settle for one who had a tiny shop. Harshit seemed very proud to do David's hair. At first, Harshit seemed to need to pace back and forth, adjusting the brushes and combs which I had moved slightly when I put down my camera and water bottle, an inch to the left, an inch to the right.

He donned a black apron, then methodically put the fan on, closed the door and pulled across a curtain. He had greasy hair and a slightly grey quiff at the front. He moved his mouth in a gummy way. He combed upwards and snipped a lot but not a lot of hair was falling to the floor. When he cut and took his hand away from the hair, his fingers kept snipping. I reckoned only 20% of snips actually cut hair. We were sitting on old metal chairs he probably inherited from his great grandfather. Loose wires hung above the mirror. There were things in the cupboard, like Synthetic Resin Adhesive, which looked like they had been there since the 70s. The longer it was going to take, the better, according to David's face. No small talk, no 'something for the weekend, sir?'.

He mixed the perfect amount of shaving cream, dunking the brush in water and getting an old pot from the cupboard. Cut-throat razor. Meticulous. Just when I thought he had finished, he moved on to do David's neck. I found myself trying to chat again.

'Is there a wine shop near here?' I asked.

'Yes,' he said, pointing to an award certificate on the wall. 'Very nice haircutting.'

Our guest house in Jaipur had an open kitchen. I use the term loosely. It was a simple area for preparing simple meals. Shelves were metal, the kind you would use in your garage. The cupboards were like old grey lockers, with the appearance of old filing cabinets. The cage-like structure around the rooftop was designed to keep monkeys out.

Breakfast time was always interesting. We tried to keep it simple. It went like this: Fried eggs, just one piece of toast, please. Black tea. Cold milk separate.

'Porridge milk' (as per the menu — basically it means porridge). Black coffee. No sugar.

The chef, wearing a small black pork pie hat, gets to work. The fried eggs are done straight away, and then left to sit behind him. Not on anything to keep it warm. (Although that seems a daft thing to say when the temperature is permanently more than 'warm'.)

The bread is put in a grubby toaster.

The black tea is produced.

Another request is made for cold milk.

The eggs and three slices of dry toast are brought to the table.

Butter and cold milk, please.

The chef was distracted while heating a pan of milk for the porridge and it has burned, so he throws it out and starts again. But he has run out of milk and shouts down through the central atrium to the floors below.

David is wondering if he will ever get his coffee. The second burner on the gas hob goes on. Water is heated and a tiny sachet of coffee is added into it.

Finally, David gets his coffee and the porridge is delivered. And I get the milk for my tea. David asks for sugar. The chef is proud that he got the order correct: 'No sugar in the coffee, sir, no sugar.'

'But can I have some for my porridge, please?'

I have given up waiting for butter and have eaten the toast.

A mouse scurries from the kitchen in through the open doors of Room 306.

A woman arrives to do the washing up. There is a small sink in the corner in which a surprising number of plates from last night's dinner have been soaking. She puts them on the floor to sort them out. And she washes the dishes by hand in cold water. They are left to drain on an equally grubby low table next to the unlidded bin.

Behind us, a mouse (is it the same one?) runs around the dusty plant pots containing faded artificial flowers.

The man who has helped serve breakfast is also the receptionist. He helps himself to the rest of the coffee in the pan and a piece of toast. Tables and chairs are left where they are, not lined up neatly after use.

We can hear the high-pitched hum of the electricity and the traffic from the main road in the distance. The courtyard is already awake with the sounds of children playing and mothers washing stainless steel dishes. And we can hear the bleat of the goat outside, tied to a tree but otherwise apparently looked after. We stop and say hello to her every day. She has fabric tied around her udder, sort of a milk nappy, presumably to catch milk or stop other goats from helping themselves.

We walked through what we fondly called Piss Alley to get to our guest house. Our room here had the whiff of wee from its toilet at all hours. David told me that it was because they have no S bends. The mistake on the first night was closing the bathroom door. The smell in the morning was even more concentrated. S bends. It's not rocket science, is it? Funnily enough though, they can do that. India has a billion-dollar space programme and yet they have not worked out toilets, water and rubbish for those here on Earth.

It's a country full of contradictions. Some of the local people told us that in the run-up to the 2019 elections, when Narendra Modi was seeking re-election, leaders had been asking people what they wanted, to which the reply was 'more temples'. Bearing in mind that India has more than two million temples — and that's just the Hindu ones — they could probably find a better way to spend the money.

By the time we reached Jaipur, we were feeling a little jaded. Jaipur, as the capital of Rajasthan, draws millions of tourists every year and is non-stop busy. Traffic is horrendous anyway but when you add in the roadworks caused by the building of a metro station, it is even worse. We took a tuk-tuk to a temple. We were not dropped off at the right one but we didn't know that until we had walked a kilometre up to the top of a hill.

The annoying thing is that, to secure the fare, a driver will say he knows where he is going. Very often, he doesn't have a clue. He will set off, only to stop several times, slowly getting closer in the general direction. He will even take a passenger clinging on to him in the front seat if he thinks they can help. One tuk-tuk driver did this. We were not impressed that he did not even bother to give way to an ambulance with a flashing light. And then he dropped us in the wrong place. We made the best of it and started walking up a hill to a very average temple. The worst thing was the girls who were begging. They pestered us up the hill. We just weren't in the mood for it. It felt like everyone was out to get us, or to get money out of us, and it was wearing thin.

What was worse, we wondered, these beggar girls or the pesky monkeys that we had been warned about? The girls, we agreed. At least the monkeys didn't see us as a never-ending supply of rupees.

We thought it might be a nice idea to visit Jhalana Panther Safari, not far from town. We shared a gypsy (jeep) with an Indian couple and their young son. It was a slow start, with monkeys, deer, some kind of antelope, a small brown and yellow woodpecker, a kingfisher. The guide knew that we wouldn't see a leopard until the sun went down, and sure enough once the light was fading we saw one a distance away, but the good zoom on our camera was more than capable of capturing it.

It would have been lovely to just sit where we were, enjoying the peace of the evening, not bothering the animals. But suddenly chaos broke out. The drivers of safari jeeps, it turns out, keep in touch with each other and report sightings at different parts of the park.

Which meant that we went at breakneck speed to another area, along with others doing the same. It was stupid. After that, it was back and forth and at one point our driver accelerated so fast around the bumpy, sandy bends that it was downright dangerous, especially with a young child in the front who was not strapped in.

Finally we stopped long enough to watch a leopard stalking a worried lone monkey who was making its bid for freedom through the tops of the trees. When we came out, not in a great mood, it was getting quite dusky. The evening air was full of dust. We noticed four dogs stretching and looking like they were about to cross the road. Few vehicles had lights on. One tuk-tuk just missed the dogs. They really weren't looking where they were going, but neither was the middle-aged motorcyclist who didn't have a helmet on. A sandy-coloured dog went under his wheels. There was a sickening sound of metal as it grated along the tarmac.

As the poor dog yelped, I flinched and turned away, my hands instinctively over my face. I couldn't bear to look. David ran over to lift up the bike. The motorcyclist was apparently unharmed, if shocked. Truth be told, we were more worried about the dog. With the bike's weight lifted off him, he raced off, pursued by two of his pack, so fast that we were never able to follow him. We couldn't even guess if he would be ok.

We walked on in silence until we found a tuk-tuk home. Where I cried.

Big ambition of a small slum girl

'The time is always right to do what's right'
—*Martin Luther King Jr*

I had never seen animals in India so happy. Pigs were snuffling around in shallow water flowing through the slum in Dehradun. The filthy water was flowing down the middle of a wide river bed. In places, rubbish had accumulated to slow it down and alter its course. There was a lot of rubbish. In fact, rubbish was this slum's business. People were picking through piles of it, scraping a meagre living. Children were being sent off for the day, out onto the busy streets to sell balloons.

From Bindal Bridge we watched as a skinny man hoisted up on to his head a huge wedge of crushed cardboard tied together with cord, and brought it up a steep dusty track to a waiting van which would take it away for recycling. We saw other adults emerging for the day, leaving the slum for the city, where they might be beggars, cleaners or vegetable sellers. Many children were left behind to fend for themselves or be looked after by older siblings. With the

Himalayas sitting hazily in the background, the slum was waking up. Washing hung around the lowest rungs of a large electricity pylon. Adults were sitting around picking nits from the hair of other adults. The tiny shops were open, selling strips of packets of crisps and sweets.

Some young children were half-naked, I presumed because they were not yet toilet trained and their parents could not afford nappies. A girl was squatting at the edge of the drop to the river, having a poo. Where there were shared toilets, they drained untreated into the river. Sanitation was their worst problem.

We were astonished by the size of the average home. A family of five were living in a basic room half the size of our kitchen back home. Due to the numbers living in close proximity with each other, sexual and domestic abuse was rife. Incidents were reducing, we were told, more because of the fear of the consequences than because they thought it was wrong. Migrants came here from Bihar, seeking a better life. How bad must it have been where they came from? There is no intention on the government's part to move the people from the slums because they would merely displace them. Where would they go?

We accepted a chai from a man who disappeared into his dark hut to make a brew. The chai was the lumpiest we had seen (we hoped it was spices rather than cockroach) and served in a thin plastic cup which was warping with the heat. The man kindly offered a plate of slices of plain white bread. David tucked in with his usual cavalier attitude to bacteria. I felt guilty for declining as we had already had breakfast. It was humbling that this man had next to nothing and yet he accepted no payment.

❧

We were visiting the riverbed slum in the company of a couple of staff members of the AASRAA Trust, whose work introduces hundreds of underprivileged children to education, keeping them off the streets and giving them basic literacy skills. They run an anti-begging campaign, offer medical care, a good midday meal and nutritious snacks, and they run their own shelter homes too.

Since they began in 2009, in response to a crisis over the welfare of children, their work has been wide-ranging and never-ending. It has often been said that the only way to combat poverty is through education. One man told us that when a child did well and managed to secure well-paid employment in medicine, law or government, there was an expectation that money would be sent back to the parents, to aunts and uncles ad infinitum to the extent that this became a significant burden and a cause of much resentment.

On a day like the day we visited, staff members would go to the slum to collect children to take them to a school. One bus filled up and another arrived to take some more. Staff also keep an eye out for those who are absent from school. It is all too easy for the children to be kept at home for work tasks or to look after a parent, or simply because their own parents have no understanding of the need for education — because they themselves never went to school.

Dehradun is not a touristy town and this was not a tour organised by a travel company in the way that we were shown Dharavi slum in Mumbai. Rather it was a personal visit to see for ourselves the work of AASRAA and see where my daughter Anouska volunteered three years earlier. I will always remember when she phoned home on her second day in floods of tears because she had seen the conditions in which the children lived. The experience helped shape her into who she is today.

There are 118 slums in Dehradun. This was a very different side to the city which has an international reputation as a centre of excellence for education. The Indian equivalent of Eton is based here. The Channel 4 TV series Indian Summer School, in which five troublesome teenagers were sent to The Doon School, was filmed in Dehradun.

The vibrant young student population was very evident — youngsters who are keen to learn and consider education a privilege.

One young girl who has learned the value of education is Manju. She was four when Anouska met her and, due to her very difficult background, she was a shy, withdrawn child. She wouldn't smile at Anouska for weeks. Once she gained her trust, however, she opened up and Anouska couldn't talk about anyone else. Manju is a shining example of the success of the AASRAA programme to enrol underprivileged children into mainstream education. She was still very shy when we met her and her older brother. After all, why should she trust two old white strangers who turn up and interrupt her school day?

We had a brief chat through an interpreter and she told us she would like to be a doctor. To one side, we asked if that was realistic. Yes, we were told, she has the potential.

Shortly before we met Manju, we went to her home in a different part of town where she lives with her grandmother. It wouldn't be appropriate to detail her family's history here, suffice to say it's been a tough start for a little girl whose parents are no longer around and it continues to be a tough life for the grandmother. As she talked to us, she welled up and her hand went instinctively to her heart. Even though she was speaking in Hindi, we felt every emotion. We guessed at her age, about 60, though she looked older. The average life expectancy for a woman in India is 65. She is illiterate.

David asked whether there was anything right now that would make her life better, thinking there could be something practical we could provide very easily. She thought for a moment, but very matter-of-factly replied no, it's all ok. But it was evident that her income did not match her expenditure. She clearly needed some help to support her two grandchildren. As we left, we gave her some money to keep her going. It was much what we paid for our train ticket from New Delhi, but it meant the world to her. She could not believe it and she choked back tears. She touched our feet as a mark of respect and we gave her a great big emotional hug.

This story began with one little girl who captured my daughter's heart. But it was her grandmother who captured mine.

We had reached Dehradun by train from New Delhi. Once again, the train service was exemplary — it departed and arrived perfectly on time, it was clean and we were given an edible breakfast and a large bottle of water. David and I were in the same carriage but for once we were not sitting next to each other. I made the following observations during the six-hour journey:

A couple are travelling with two young children but they seem to have booked only two seats. While the two seats to my left remain available, the man and young son sit there. He tries to change a nappy. He passes a drink across me. He passes the child across me.

A man (behind, right) coughs. Not just a polite cough but something deeper, wetter and disgusting.

A woman burps.

Someone starts snoring loudly.

Chai is served in individual flasks, with biscuits.

At one stop, two women arrive for the seats next to me. They insist on putting large bags under seats. My elderly grey-haired neighbour is very mismatched, pink floral top, crazy patterned bottoms, grey tank top, pink socks and flip flops. She gets out what looks like a yellow bandana, ties it around her hand, seems to bless it, puts a floral scarf around that and keeps her hand raised. Maybe it is like worry beads.

Another belch rumbles out from a woman.

The woman behind me lets out three belches in a row. The first one transforms seamlessly into an exhalation of 'ohhhh'. Not an embarrassed 'oh', just a relieved if slightly painful one.

After breakfast the belching begins in earnest. Women all around me let it out as if in training for a new category in the Olympics.

The man behind does a combined cough/sigh in a strange way almost like he's just been stabbed.

All I am doing is trying to read my book. And crossing my fingers it's not the turn of farting next.

Breakfast has revived everyone and strangers are striking up conversations all round. Some women are laughing with a man with a long greying beard and friendly face. He is sporting a black and white checked bandana.

To my left a woman comes out with a belch which rivals Elf. I nearly get the giggles.

Behind me the 'ohhhh' belch repeats itself.

My neighbour puts her bobble hat into her camouflage handbag and gets out her smartphone to put on some Indian music. It's strangely relaxing.

I glance over and smile and she smiles back. The music is coming from a video on YouTube which shows a baby-god with a revolving halo behind it and what looks like a parrot swinging on a banana. Her head starts moving to the music, her hand gesticulating.

Her socks have big toes. These are socks designed for flip-flops.

She crosses her leg, ankle to knee. The other foot taps to the music.

We establish that she is going to Haridwar, an ancient Hindu pilgrimage city.

A breakfast tray crashes to the floor. A little girl to my right, left alone for two minutes while Mum goes to the loo, looks up with a 'It wasn't me' look. She leaves it there. Mum returns and she leaves it there too.

Station by station, the train empties, leaving it blissfully quiet and calm.

David's journey went like this...

I love trains, particularly dirty, old Indian trains.

Despite this train's relative antiquity, it was clean and comfortable. When I took up my position in the middle of three seats, I only had a Granny-ji on my right to talk to but she did not speak a word of English.

Just before we left, a young girl of about 20 claimed the other seat next to me. I busied myself looking at photos on my iPad and she started reading a paperback written in English.

When chai was delivered, I passed her tray to her. When the breakfast arrived, ditto. She thanked me in English. I continued to look at my photos and, before long, her curiosity got the better of her and she asked where I was from. Grateful for my iPad, I touched on the map app and showed her my island home between France and England.

She told me her name was Pallavi and for the rest of the journey we chatted on and off about many different topics from travel to politics, arranged marriage, religion, toilets, wifi, head wobbles, Indian manners and queuing. We spoke about women's emancipation in a still patriarchal society and about the appalling caste system which, though often denied, is alive and well.

Pallavi's older sister was getting married later in the month, an arranged marriage. In India, she told me, the bride's parents will often go into huge debt to throw an ostentatious party that can last for days. Elaborate costumes, horses, catering and photography, all because everyone else does it and they have to be seen to do the same or face shame and ridicule. Then there is the payment of a dowry. The newlyweds will be expected to live with the groom's family and there will be many demands on their income.

Pallavi was travelling to Dehradun for an interview. She hoped to persuade the Department of Defence that she was worthy of their scholarship. Higher education has to be paid for in India and a scholarship was her only hope of realising her dreams. She told me that before she reaches 30 her parents will select a husband for her and she will be expected to forgo her career to keep home and produce a family, as per ancient tradition.

My new friend was kind enough to seem interested in my family and our recent travels.

Pallavi was an intelligent, articulate and well-educated young woman. We agreed that India, the place of her birth and the place I love, is in transition. Its problems are many, huge and seemingly insurmountable. But her generation is the hope for India.

I only wish that we were young enough to return in 30 years' time to see what progress has been made.

World Toilet Day is held every year on 19 November. It gave us a chance to reflect on the fact that although more people than ever before have access to a toilet, at least 522 million people in India still defecate in the open.

It was at a railway station in Mumbai that we had seen a sign with a quote from Gandhi: 'If we do not keep our back yards clean, our swaraj will have a foul stench.' When he was in South Africa, he had seen poor men carrying buckets of excreta on their heads. On that day he vowed to clean his own toilet. In fact, he would later fall out with his wife when he told her she would have to take her turn in cleaning the toilet, rather than leave it to someone from a lower caste, an untouchable.

In 2014, on Gandhi's birthday, India's Prime Minister Narendra Modi launched the $31 billion Swachh Bharat, or Clean India, mission with the aim of constructing 111 million toilets in five years. By 2019, the country should have been free of open defecation. Better sanitation should reduce the incidence of diarrhoea, still the second leading cause of death in children under five. We read somewhere that of India's population of more than 1.3 billion, 84% have unlimited wifi and yet 54% have no access to a toilet and 6% don't know where tomorrow's food is coming from.

We encountered four kinds of toilet in India — the western loo, the Indian squat toilet, a combination of the two so you get what looks like a squatting ledge but at a toilet seat level, and, worst of all really, the western loo which has no seat.

Indians do not like the use of toilet paper. They prefer to use a jet of water, claiming that it is more hygienic. In our homestays in Madurai, Udaipur and Dehradun, no toilet paper was provided nor was it forthcoming. In Madurai we couldn't find any on sale in the town, so we had to make do. We had to time things so we could have a shower immediately afterwards or we would have to use the power hose on the wall. We were never quite sure whether the hose was supposed to replace a toilet brush or toilet paper.

For a woman, the seatless toilets were the worst. You hover at first, but can't relax enough to release. So you dip to a point where the minimum amount of flesh meets the porcelain, enough to get a result, before hovering again. I just hoped my back didn't lock in this position. And sometimes, if there was a seat and you lifted it, you came to expect it to release a dozen mosquitoes into the air.

My favourite toilet moment had been at a motorway service station in Sri Lanka, where we had to pay 20 rupees to go in. A woman stamped a little ticket and handed it over. David looked at her wryly and said: 'That's not big enough to wipe my arse, is it?'

Never give up

'Everything will be all right in the end. If it's not all right, it is not yet the end'

—*Sonny Kapoor in The Best
Exotic Marigold Hotel*

Sink or swim. That's what I said it was. Make or break. I had often joked that sending my daughter away to Borneo was like sending her off to boot camp, the kind of American-style brutal regime that makes tough teenagers cry.

I was close to giving up on her. Since leaving school with a small handful of GCSEs, Anouska had spent three years being a quitter. At least, this is how I saw it as a mother. She quit further education college, she quit a work progression scheme, she quit any briefly held part-time work. She seemed unable to apply herself to anything. Her self-esteem was almost non-existent. She had no money of her own and therefore no way of treating herself to some nice clothes. More than anything, what bothered me was the laziness and the lying. She didn't make an effort to change her lifestyle, she could be full of good intentions but seemed to lack the ability to put them into effect, and there was no intention of starting to listen to me, that's for sure.

Crisis was reached when she was self-harming and I just didn't know what to do for the best. I mean, when you see your beautiful 18-year-old daughter sitting next to two knives and a pair of scissors, streaks of blood on her arms and streams of black mascara down her face, as a parent you do wonder where you went wrong. Shouldn't an 18-year-old be having the time of her life?

We tried to get a diagnosis of something, of anything, to no avail. She was offered counselling, but she could not bring herself to engage with anyone. On the day that the UK was celebrating Prince William's marriage to Kate Middleton, I was reeling by a message she sent to me saying that she wanted to die. Mental health wasn't as big an issue as it is today. I might have read in newspapers about the increasing awareness of it. Here it was playing out before my very eyes, but I don't think I knew it at the time.

I wonder now whether I could have been more sympathetic, more supportive, whether I could have taken a different tack. I wish I had been taught emotional resilience much earlier in parenthood.

I would often find myself complaining to friends as we stomped the north coast of Jersey. Two of them had teenagers who had been on a Raleigh International expedition. It sounded tough but exciting. A challenge for 'regular' kids. Could my daughter cope? Would it be too much? I showed her the website. She jumped at the chance, even though she thought that Borneo was in Africa. I stressed to her that this would be no holiday. There would be vaccinations (she hated needles), bugs the size of her hand (she screamed at moths), and sleeping in a hammock in the middle of a jungle (she slept with the light on).

We committed to fundraising the £3,150 required by the charity. It often felt like it was my project, not hers, such was the amount of effort she put in willingly. Requests for raffle prizes, thank-you letters, organising meetings, all were done by her, but only after exhausting cajoling on my part.

But then, we reached the target, the flights were booked and suddenly we were on the plane to London together. I had always said I would get her as far as Heathrow. What I hadn't told her was that it was so I could make sure she did not miss the flight, deliberately or otherwise. Along with a few other tearful parents, I left her as she headed off through security. She looked a little nervous but no more so than any of the other venturers.

As soon as I got on the coach back to Gatwick (you can't fly to Jersey from Heathrow), I bawled my eyes out, for pretty much the whole hour. At the airport I decided to enjoy a quiet lunch by myself and the waitress asked if I was going somewhere nice. I started trying to explain but I choked on my words and could say no more.

I got home to discover peace and quiet, no added mess in the kitchen, no doors slamming at 3 am, no arguments about staying out and no requests for money. I could leave my bedroom door unlocked.

The venturers all come back different people, the Raleigh representative told parents at the airport, empowered, able to take on the world. I admit I thought they were going to have their work cut out. I delighted in following the blogs about the expedition. I spotted Anouska in several pictures, in a group called Alpha 2, installing a gravity-fed water system. She was as remote as remote could be, a four-hour drive from base camp plus a two-hour trek uphill. And there she was, smiling and looking healthier already. Surely getting away from hours hunched over a laptop, junk food, fizzy drinks, alcohol, social media and some toxic friends was going to have beneficial results. That and the fact that she would be labouring in intense heat and humidity from dawn until dusk. I never doubted it. I just wondered how long it would take.

After the first project was complete, the venturers returned to base camp, where they could contact the outside world for the first time in three weeks. She phoned home. She sounded so positive, so grown up. She said she wanted to travel and teach English as a foreign language to children. She thanked me for everything (and has since apologised many times for her rough years). At this point I relaxed. It was going to work out. Her journey through life had taken a different path, an exciting one full of possibilities. I always knew she had potential. On good days I hadn't lost sight of the real her, the loving, caring, funny girl with a Miranda Hart sense of humour.

Her second project was to create conservation trails for eco-tourism, and the third phase gave her her toughest personal challenge – an 11-day trek through the rainforest, carrying kit and rations and setting up camp each night. Later, Anouska admitted that she had been quite lazy in the first phase, but by the second she was learning a lot about herself as well as how Raleigh brought everyone together.

'I started to volunteer for everything. I enjoyed cleaning and cooking and I really enjoyed working as part of a team,' she said. 'I think I noticed what Raleigh was all about when we were trekking. You have a lot of time to think on trek and one day it just hit me that I had been in Borneo for 10 weeks and I had not given up. I felt so great. I had achieved something.'

She said that she got used to the bites and stings from leeches, bees, red ants and mosquitoes and she even learned to appreciate homesickness. Anouska added that she felt like a completely different person. 'I felt absolutely amazing and healthy,' she said. 'Raleigh is all about leadership and change. The villagers in Borneo that we met may not have clean water or a lot of food, but they seem so grateful for what they have.'

Midway through the expedition, she sent me a message which made everything fit into place. She was, she said, happy.

To cut a long story short, the Raleigh experience was life-changing. Anouska applied herself from that moment on. She worked hard waitressing for a year, got a Teaching English as a Foreign Language qualification under her belt, and then — because she couldn't in that academic year secure a college place to further her studies — she decided to go to Dehradun for three months. She had never been to India before and I am not sure she really knew what to expect. But off she went for another exciting adventure.

It wasn't without its challenges. It was colder than she expected, she had some awful mosquito bites, she developed a nasty boil on her elbow that required medical attention, and… well, it turned out that hardly anyone spoke English. There you go, I said, that's what you're there for. She was volunteering with the AASRAA Trust. Her accommodation and food were basic, her bed was rock solid, she had access to a bucket and tap for washing, there was no toilet paper and there was not much respite from porridge and rice.

On the second day, she was taken to the riverbed slum. She had never seen anything like it. In an article that was published in our local paper, she described the experience:

'I have never seen so many pigs in my life, all filthy, all running around in dirt, it was heaven to them. Rubbish absolutely everywhere and the river wasn't a normal colour. It was completely polluted and barefoot children would walk through it to find things to recycle or sell. It breaks my heart to even think about it. The emotions I felt walking through every day to collect the children were like nothing I've ever experienced before. The smells were absolutely disgusting and I don't know how they can deal with it every day.

'I was shocked to hear about the backgrounds of some of the children. Some children are raped, beaten, threatened or made to be slaves but at school you wouldn't know that. It must have been a relief for many of them to get away, to go to school and see what they were capable of.'

Manju was four when Anouska met her. A very withdrawn child, she wouldn't smile and she didn't speak. Slowly, Anouska coaxed her out of her shell by drawing pictures and making funny faces on videos on her phone.

'She used to stare at me, like most of the children did, but she looked at me with such disgust and didn't speak to me until my last month. One day, I was helping out with a maths class. As I kept playfully repeating her name "Manju, Manju, Manju", something lit in her. After that, she played with me every lunchtime until I left. I remember the morning that she ran up to me for a hug, shouting "Annie DeeDee" which means "sister". It melted my heart, and she would run up to me every day after that to hug me. Manju was a cheeky young girl, full of mischief and fun.'

When it came to leaving Dehradun, Anouska found it difficult to leave Manju behind. Once she was home, she raised some money to support the family and vowed to return, much like I did after my three-month adventure at around the same age. Anouska came home just in time for a family wedding and her 21st birthday, and went on to get her college place, later gaining great grades in her childcare studies.

She has also put in hundreds of voluntary hours with a charity which encourages and empowers young leaders. She often finds herself talking to young teenagers about issues which she herself faced.

Sigh.

If only a parent could be told not to worry. Everything will indeed be all right in the end.

It's enough to make you sick

'If you don't like seeing pictures of violence towards animals being posted, you need to help stop the violence, not the pictures'

—*Johnny Depp*

On Day 149, 27 November, I shared on Facebook a link to the two-hour Australian documentary Dominion.

There is no such thing as humane or ethical murder. Just watched Dominion. There is footage of some hideous bastards but most of the actual processes of the animal industry shown here are legal. Don't kid yourself what suffering happens for the meat industry wherever you are in the world.

God, was I angry. We had watched the hard-hitting documentary, which questions the morality of humans' dominion over the animal kingdom. It was tough to watch. Even the four-minute trailer makes me cry. It is freely available online.

Once you have seen it, you can't forget it. I was upset but now that I had opened my eyes, more than anything, I was angry. I felt a greater passion than I had felt about anything in years. I wanted to do something about it. I wanted to shout from the rooftops: Why are we still eating animals? What gives anyone the right to kill these sentient beings? Why do we see it as different, the pork on our plate, the dogs killed in China or Vietnam? Why do we see it as ok, just because we like the taste? Why do we care about bull-fighting, seal culling and smoking beagles, but we can quite happily eat surf and turf? How can anyone say they're an animal lover while tucking into a bacon roll? Why do we get angry with trophy hunters, but continue to eat roast lamb?

I was berating myself for not making the connection sooner. Once I was home, I could hardly believe my eyes walking around the supermarket. Whole swathes of products that I would now ignore. Shelf after shelf of products that have used animals in some way. The fish counter — fabulous fish that should be swimming in the sea. Dairy produce — the torment of the cows and their calves pulled apart hours after birth and the superfluous heifers sent for slaughter simply for being born male. Eggs — the male chicks which are deemed so useless that they are tossed straight into the grinder alive. The meat counter — where I just see death. Dead animals, carved up by a butcher's knife. What horrors did that animal suffer as it was taken in a truck on a journey to the slaughterhouse? How did it feel when it was desperate to escape? Was its murder quick?

Some methods of killing are not swift at all. Chickens, for example, are hung upside down by their feet and in their struggle might move in such a way as to miss the thing that should stun them, so it ends up being particularly cruel when their throat is slit.

I was astounded to learn that there are nearly 800 mega-farms in the UK — intensive factory farming in pretty much every county. It's on a large scale and it's increasing.

In our culture, using animals for our own purposes is ingrained. Children's books are full of farms and zoos. It's what we are taught at school. 'Milk is good for you, essential for the growth of bones.' 'Go to work on an egg.' It's backed up by our parents. We owe much of our thinking to slick marketing by multi-million pound industries.

My sister, who lives in Canada, was ahead of her time in advocating for veganism. I am not sure why her message didn't get through to us sooner. Maybe we were just wilfully ignorant. On one visit to Jersey we took her out for an Indian meal, in the days well before the word vegan was established on menus. Having quizzed the waiter at length, she realised that there was very little that she could eat and it only reinforced David's belief that, if he were a vegan, eating out would be a boring, embarrassing nightmare. It seemed there were too many extreme restrictions and, for him, having to make a fuss when ordering food was out of the question.

But now it's changing fast. Producers react to market trends and every week, it seems, there are more choices for vegetarians and vegans. Greggs have successfully produced a vegan pasty and KFC have come up with a vegan burger.

Vegans want to see an end to the farming of animals for food but we have to be reasonable and pragmatic. Huge multi-million pound industries are not going to change overnight, but businesses will have to adapt to consumer trends, just like the tobacco industry had to. Farming has become just too intensive, leading to huge industrial farms where as many animals as possible occupy the available space, milk yields are unnaturally high, and chickens are fed so much that they grow to a weight that can barely be supported by their scrawny little legs.

We, the consumers, have a huge part to play in animal welfare. If we demand cheap meat, some poor creature will be paying a very high price. Is it at least better to choose meat that has been ethically reared? The pig you eat may have been kept well. Hell, it may even have been tucked up in bed under a feather duvet, but ultimately it has been exploited to serve your food choices and there is simply no humane way to kill an animal that doesn't want to be killed.

When we did finally find our own path to veganism we came to the painful realisation that Nicola had been right all along. We had been those naive, irritating people who say: 'But bacon?' and 'If God didn't want us to eat animals, why did he make them taste so good?'

Veganism now seems like a no-brainer even though for 54 years we were happy carnivores who claimed to love animals but still ate them. We had had no idea that life was going to take us this way.

From Dehradun we were heading for the hills. Our route took us up to Mussoorie and Shimla before we reached our northernmost point, Amritsar. The winding roads were not for the fainthearted. We were increasingly convinced that not all Indian motorists have passed driving tests or indeed had any lessons. One driver, whose name we took to be Ashishit for that was emblazoned on his windscreen, over-took in odd places and was easily distracted picking his ears or smiling inanely at his music player. Most taxis didn't have functional seat belts in the back, and most drivers used

IT'S ENOUGH TO MAKE YOU SICK

their mobile phones, something that I detest. One time we were coming down a hill and we had already seen a local bus overtake at speed on a blind bend, when the young driver took a call. He held his phone in his left hand, and when he needed to change gear, his right hand came across his body to reach the gear stick.

'I'm going to have to say something,' I muttered to David.

Out of the blue, David thumped the back of the seat so hard that it made the driver look around, startled, and then we both had to shout at him to keep his eyes on the road ahead. We berated him for using his phone and reminded him of the laws of his country. He didn't do it again.

Most drivers expect a tip. With many drivers who used their phone, we kept a typical British silence but we hatched a new plan. During the journey we would hook out a bit of scrap paper from my rucksack and write: *TIP: Do not use your phone while driving.*

And we folded it up with the exact rupees for the fare. I have no idea if it was lost on them but it made us feel better. What didn't make us feel particularly well was the effect of the winding roads, at speed, with a degree of fear, which sometimes went on for four or five hours. One such journey made David throw up. We had stopped for a break, the driver went off for a fag and something to chew and spit, and I went to stroke the nearest friendly dog. I noticed that David stayed in the car. Luckily we still had a few airline sick bags on us and he reached for one of those. Back on the road, the driver heard one more chuck before he realised that he needed to slow down. (That and the fact that David warned: 'If you don't slow down, you're going to get a liquid laugh all down your neck.') Truth was, we were all desperate for the journey to be over as quickly as possible.

Apart from that, it was sickening just how healthy David was throughout the journey. He could eat pretty much anything with no adverse effect and he didn't even get the runs.

'Perfect arsehole, my love,' he observed.

I'm saying nothing.

One of the things we loved about India was seeing the very different character of each state. Shimla brought the cool, clear air of the mountains, the colonial influence in the buildings and, something we had not seen anywhere else, the pedestrianisation of the main town area. No tuk-tuks or motorbikes jostling for space. No cars hooting constantly. Just blissful peace and quiet.

Shimla appeared not to have a litter problem in the main area around Christ Church and there were signs telling people not to smoke or spit in public. The fact that cars cannot go up the streets, however, does mean that there is much work for delivery men to haul ridiculous quantities of goods up the hills to hotels, restaurants and shops. These wiry, dusty men carry way too much, such as five boxed large TV screens, two gas cylinders, or a huge sack of potatoes with a large box of apples balanced on the top. Is it a silly question to ask why they can't invest in a sack truck?

We enjoyed a morning exploring a temple at the top of a very steep hill. We took the cable car, fancily called the Jakhu Ropeway, something that actually made me more nervous than the Indian roads. India's safety record isn't exactly reassuring and I decided that I might have more chance of survival if I sat stock still and didn't look down into the treetops or up at the cable itself.

We enjoyed a pleasant hour or so walking around Jakhu Temple and sitting in the sun in the gardens. There's not much there other than a giant Hannuman monkey god erected in 2000 and some pesky real monkeys which we'd been warned about. It was amusing to watch them grab food from people. Some people carried sticks to ward them off. One monkey nicked a man's sunglasses and swiftly bounced back up to a roof with them. A stall-holder went over, just as he probably does every day, and threw a piece of coconut up. The monkey effortlessly caught it and promptly threw the glasses to the man. It was a fair exchange.

At 2,453 m, the temple had provided us with the highest point in our whole trip. We decided that we would walk back down the hill but couldn't quite find the right pathway. So we asked a tourist who was wearing a lovely sky blue kurti. In the brief conversation, we established that she was travelling with the same company that we used on our first visit to India and Nepal just four years before. Well, we said, your rep doesn't happen to be Jayne, does it? Yes, it did!

When we got back to our hotel we emailed Jayne to see if she had time to say hello. Not only did she get my email in time, but also she said yes. The next day, we met in the main street and enjoyed a quick coffee catching up at a cute little café which we had made our local.

In passing, just out of interest, we happened to ask whether the company still included elephant riding in its itineraries. Disappointingly, it does. She didn't seem to think this was a problem. It wasn't the time or place to go into it further, so we left it at that. As we emerged onto the street and said our goodbyes, I could feel another letter coming on.

Here's an idea. Instead of counting sheep when you can't sleep at night, count the number of animals which were killed today. See them going into the slaughterhouse. Imagine what will happen to them next.

According to the Humane Slaughter Association, approximately 7,100 cattle, 27,400 pigs, 38,350 sheep and lambs, 219,180 fish and 2.6 million birds are slaughtered for human consumption.

Just in the UK.

Every single day.

That's enough to keep anyone awake at night.

Temples, toilets and tampons

'Of all the evils for which man has made himself responsible, none is so degrading, so shocking or so brutal as his abuse of the better half of humanity; the female sex'

—*Mahatma Gandhi*

It's not every day that you find yourself surrounded by hundreds of Indian women, young and old, dancing to Jai Ho, in front of an audience of several thousand. The Attari-Wagah ceremony at the India-Pakistan border has become something of a must-do for any visitor to Amritsar. It is just 20 km from the holy city.

I am not sure when it changed from being a sombre beating retreat ceremony, if indeed it ever was, to being a patriotic spectacle enjoyed by so many. It starts with women from the crowd lining up to take their turn walking around with the Indian flag. An officer from the Border Security Force reminded us of Freddie Mercury. Dressed in camouflage gear (not that effective, we saw him a mile off), he acted like crowd control and warm-up man combined, getting the crowds to cheer louder and applaud on time.

Then the music started and women danced on the street, arms in the air, a celebratory atmosphere. Every age, every type of clothing, from full decorated sari to jeans and T-shirt. I decided to join in, even though my dancing is appalling. I jumped up and down a bit, followed other women's moves with their arms and smiled a lot. It was joyful.

I was not entirely sure why it is only women who are allowed to dance at the ceremony.

Our young Indian guide Rabia (who was also our driver that day, the best we had had in six months and the only female driver in that time) was quick to point out the discrimination on the Pakistan side of the border, where men and women were segregated.

This was Rabia's 72nd border ceremony, not that she was counting, and she had not tired of it yet. She explained that the Border Security Force dogs would perform for us. They walked through with their officers and 'bowed' to one side of the street, maybe to the flag or something. I was quite glad that was all the performing they did. One was a handsome Alsatian befitting of his post, the other two were short labradors who looked like they had eaten a chapati or two too many.

After this, the proper ceremony got under way. This was the serious side. Well, as serious as it gets. Army officers in beige uniforms and rooster-like headgear marched up and down, sometimes goose-stepping in a Basil Fawlty ('Don't mention the war') way and stomping on the ground in time with the beat of the music. Could they really be fighting men?

Another officer was making loooooong calls on the microphone, to which the crowd, whipped into a frenzy of nationalism, would respond with shouts of 'Hindustan'.

On the other side of the border, we could see the Pakistan crowd, much smaller than ours and not so noisy. India and

Pakistan then had a competition to see who would be first to untie a knot on a rope holding their country's flag. Pakistan won. We didn't care because we couldn't quite see the detail as we were looking straight into the setting sun.

All this is now a peaceful and fun way to mark the line between the two countries and to formally close the border each night. At the end of the ceremony, the crowds dispersed in a slow, contented way, like they do after a large music concert, small flags in hand, 'I love my India' baseball caps on, the saffron, white and green of the Indian flag painted on faces.

Earlier, we had been to the Partition Museum and the gardens at Jallianwala Bagh, the site of the grim massacre of unarmed civilians in April 1919 at the hands of a British General, to learn more about the violent time India faced in becoming independent of Great Britain and the creation of Pakistan in 1947.

Both are within a short walk of the stunning Golden Temple, which buzzes with Sikhs who have come from far and wide to be here. It is estimated that 100,000 people visit it on a daily basis but it didn't feel overcrowded. It was just a glorious combination of colour, music, worship, friendly people and surprisingly few western tourists. It felt alive and spiritual, as did I.

Anyone watching the Attari-Wagah spectacle might think that women in India have a happy, easy time of it and yet nothing could be further from the truth. This is a hugely patriarchal society, a place where you still need government messages painted on walls telling people that baby girls are just as important as boys.

Before we went to India together the first time, David and I had read about 23-year-old Jyoti Singh, who was tortured, gang-raped and beaten with an iron bar on a bus in Delhi in December 2012. The iron bar caused such devastating injuries that one of the attackers was able to pull out her intestines through her vagina. She died from her injuries two weeks later.

It was a sickening case which made headlines around the world and has since been the subject of a series on Netflix. We had already bought our tickets to Delhi for our 2014 trip but this made us stop and think. Should we boycott India?

It just so happened that around that time we were attending a talk by a well-known TV travel presenter and afterwards we asked him what he thought. He reasoned that no one would even notice if we just didn't go. We might as well carry on, he said, perhaps talk to people about the issues while there, or indeed write something.

Looking into it now, it would appear that all that's really changed is that they have got rid of curtains on the buses.

Attitudes to women have not really shifted. Not enough, anyway. The men who raped Jyoti, including the bus driver, took the view that she was there for them to do with her what they wished. The attorney for the defence voiced a popularly held view that a young woman out with her boyfriend at that time of night bore responsibility for what happened to her.

One thing that does happen now is that taxi drivers who want to renew their licence must sit through 'gender sensitisation' classes. In Delhi we saw stickers on the back of tuktuks declaring: 'Along with my taxi, I also drive a campaign to end violence against women.' Although it means that the driver has attended the class, it doesn't necessarily mean they agree with it.

Social media is inevitably one of the driving forces for change in India and, hopefully, change for the better. It's in the cities where there is greater potential for a clash. This is where women are more independent, modern and wester-nised, but many of the taxi and tuk-tuk drivers have come from rural areas, where there is less education and more tra-ditional views of women.

Gandhi was truly ahead of his time. Although he died in 1948, his spirit is still pervasive throughout India and we enjoyed visiting a couple of museums dedicated to his life and work. He led his country to independence through his campaign of non-violent civil disobedience. Many of his pronouncements on caste, the environment, health and edu-cation are increasingly vindicated by a generation who seem more attuned to his message than their fathers ever were.

And his view of women? He said: 'There is no occasion for women to consider themselves subordinate or inferior to men.'

One of the strangest things in India was seeing signs outside temples which said that women could not enter if they had their period.

Shortly after we returned home, there was a protest in Thiruvananthapuram in Kerala against a centuries-old ban on menstruating women entering the temple. These kind of situations astonish me because, let's face it, it wasn't a god who imposed the ban. It was a man.

In India, there continues to be a huge stigma about men-struation. According to the Women Economic Forum (www.wef.org.in), many mothers don't educate their daughters about why they have periods so they live in the dark about hygiene and what is happening to their bodies. It quotes an astonishing statistic: Only 12 per cent of women and girls in India use sanitary pads. There is no reference to tampons. One can only wonder what they use, if anything, or whether it means they just stay at home, which begs the question: How many hours of school and work are they missing every month?

David and I recalled a conversation we had had with a woman who was well educated and in a respectable job and yet in her own home she was not allowed in the kitchen to cook the family dinner while she had her period.

We noticed that tampons were not generally available, certainly not south of Mumbai. Small packets could be found in touristy areas like Pushkar but there were none to be had in the supermarket in Alleppey. I had noticed that there was a lack of tampons because I had been keeping an eye out for a small supply. Being menopausal, everything had become bloody unpredictable. As it happens, I can now be sure that the last time I was actually in need of one was in the middle of a seven-hour journey down the Mekong. In the middle of nowhere. On a river. Great.

In Amritsar, we were back to what we fondly referred to as the 'real India', the noisy, hooting, dirty chaos of tuk-tuks, cycle rickshaws, fruit barrows, beggars, barking dogs, and men pushing crazy loads on sets of ancient wheels. Many a time we went down grey grungy alleys, occasionally brightened with colourful fabric shops, with their dangling power cables, crumbling pavements, cows and dogs scavenging in the piles of rubbish, and observed that it felt like it belonged to another century.

And yet, in some ways, the country can be quite progressive. It was here that we found a McDonalds which is entirely vegetarian. I hesitated to go in because I was not sure that I wanted to support a company which kills millions of cows every year. (There's a great quote attributed to McDonalds online which basically says 'we don't kill cows' because, their argument goes, someone else does the slaughtering. Hmm.) But we needed refreshment and curiosity got the better of us. We went in, ordered a veggie burger and headed upstairs for the view over the street.

We didn't know it at the time but we had walked into McDonalds' first entirely meat-free restaurant, which opened in 2013. It's not far from the Golden Temple, where consumption of meat is forbidden. For many people in India, vegetarianism is a way of life, with 42% of people not eating meat, fish or eggs. According to www.vegetarians. co.nz, India contains more vegetarians than the rest of the world combined – roughly half a billion people.

The fact that McDonalds is running a meat-free restaurant just makes me think… If they can do it here, they can do it anywhere.

We started wondering whether giants like McDonalds and KFC could soon be leading the way in meat-free alternatives and developing meat-free burgers, sausages and nuggets which are so good you wouldn't know you weren't eating meat. A McDonalds without the suffering. It is entirely possible.

I remember Amritsar as the place that rioting broke out a few days after I visited in 1983. Not that I was aware of it at the time, there being no social media. My mum had a copy of my rough itinerary on her coffee table but, with no Facebook or easy way to stay in touch, she had no idea where I was when she read the reports in the newspaper and she had no way of contacting me. It would be three weeks later, through my oblivious chatty Air Mail letter, that she would know I was ok.

In a way, I suppose, some of her worries materialised. When I arrived home, I weighed about 45 kg, and strawberries and Jersey Royals made me vomit. One week later, I had an epileptic fit. It was only then that I realised I had been experiencing petit mal episodes for the previous year or two. It had been pure luck that I hadn't had one while posing for photos on the edge of precarious drops at the top of castle walls.

This time around, I am not sure Mum was any more relaxed about me being away for months on the other side of the world but at least she learned how to use FaceTime independently, even if she did sometimes spend the whole conversation with her picture locked upside down.

'The way to avoid [being bitter and angry] is to see fare negotiation for what it truly is: a pantomime. A game. A source of fun.'

In his book Delirious Delhi, Dave Prager describes Indian ways such as bartering as a pantomime. Oh yes he does. Armed with that thought, we found it a good way to cope with the everyday challenges of getting through another day in India.

You have to play the game... the bartering and negotiating for just about anything, choosing from a menu which never has what you want, crossing the chaotic roads where everyone is jostling for an extra centimetre of space, catching a tuk-tuk, interpreting the head-shake, posing for photos with the holidaying Indians who come up and ask 'One selfie please, ma'am?'

Nowhere was the farce more evident than in our Amritsar hotel. OYO is a brand of budget-range hotels throughout India, with the emphasis very much on the word budget. We had the misfortune to stay in one or two, leading us to rename them OH-NO. The email confirming our booking stressed that we would most certainly be given the 100% OYO experience on arrival. Regrettably, they were right.

We noted a few examples:

Hotel 1, day 1: We asked at 7.45 am where we could get breakfast. The reply was that it was all room service, from 8.30. We placed our order, thinking it would be ready for 8.30. We went to a nearby hotel to use their wifi as there was none (none!) in our hotel. We first had to wake the man who was sleeping behind the desk in the reception area. We returned to our hotel at 8.30. The chef trotted off to his domain and eventually we got food at 9.10 am. All that for a boiled egg and toast.

Hotel 1, day 2: We ordered boiled eggs and toast at 8 am. While we waited, we read books and fed the monkey outside. At 9.15 breakfast was delivered with a flourish: A stale tomato and cucumber sandwich.

Hotel 2, day 1: We tried to order coffee, tea and fried eggs. We got two orders of eggs instead of one, four slices of toast, not one. The coffee and tea proved to be particularly complicated because we asked for it with no sugar and separate milk (furrowed brows every time). The young man in a black suit tried so hard, bless him, but he really was like a young Basil Fawlty apprentice, right down to the moustache.

At the third OYO hotel, the main man Arjun (Arji-Bhaji, as we liked to call him) came over to see what we were doing in the restaurant. When I say restaurant, it was a room furnished only with some basic tables and chairs. It had bare white walls which featured some large black patches of damp. A hole had formed in the ceiling where there had been a leak but no one seemed aware of it, let alone worried about it. Water was still dripping down one wall.

Arji-Bhaji mosied on over and did something that David absolutely hates. He lurked right behind him and stared at David's iPad screen to see what he was doing. He didn't try to start a conversation. He just stared.

He's behind you…

'Yes? Can I help you?' David asked.

Arji-Bhaji's English wasn't good enough to embark on a conversation so off he went. Later, with some trepidation, we informed him we would be leaving at 4 am to catch a train. I had two questions. Would the front doors be unlocked? And could we get a tuk-tuk round here at that time of the morning?

'Train. No problem. Check out.'

I repeated my questions.

'Will the front door be open? Can we get out?'

'Tuk-tuk. Station. No problem.'

And so it went on. Sometimes we started talking so sarcastically that I crossed my fingers they didn't understand how rude we were starting to be. That same evening Arji-Bhaji came over to confirm when we would check out. 'Yes, yes, tonight,' we said.

'Tip,' he said.

Excuse me?

'Tip. I finish at 11 pm and start at 7 am.' The inference being… so you might not see me again. 'Tip.'

Hmmm, well, let me see.

You know what? I have a tip for you. I have a few actually, seeing as you asked. Tips are discretionary, for good service. All you have done is your job. And not a very good one at that. You have not gone above and beyond any measurable measure of service. You are surly, slimy, and truth be told we don't actually like you. You stand there in your scruffy trousers, grey shirt and woolly tank-top, but you haven't helped us once. Your rubbish budget OYO hotel has had shite wifi which we cannot get in our room but we can occasionally get a signal in this awful space you call a restaurant and you haven't attempted to stop that leak down the wall, and you don't even give us a small complimentary bottle of water each day, and the other day when we asked if we could have cornflakes instead of some 'idli-shit' or instead of 'butter-toast' you said no. No! Well, we could but not if we wanted the free tea and coffee as well. EVEN THOUGH CORNFLAKES IS THE SAME PRICE ON THE MENU AS BUTTER-TOAST and we had that with tea and coffee the day before. And by the way, your butter tastes horrible. And when we asked for toilet paper, you gave us a packet of hotel-branded napkins. And your shower is rubbish. We let it run for 15 minutes to see if it will warm up. It doesn't get beyond tepid. And you put us in a room on the road-side of the hotel, next to not one road but two, one on top of the other, one of which is a major highway. And the traffic honks all day and the fumes in our room, where there is single glazing and loose windows, MUST BE EFFING KILLING US. And have I mentioned that you woke me up the other morning when you phoned our room and said something in Hindi? I mean, it's not like there are any other white people in your hotel right now, and you got the wrong number, without so much as an apology. Or maybe you were just being evil and winding us up? And by the way, our door handle is falling off. And when I washed my socks and left them to dry on the windowsill, in the morning they were covered – COVERED! – in little reddish-brown ants. And Sir – SIR – it is very rude to stand behind someone and stare at their screen. And you have the AUDACITY to ask for a tip.

Ah, all those things I wish I had said. I looked in my purse. There was no way I was giving him a 500-rupee note (just over a fiver). I didn't have anything smaller. And while I looked, I decided. No, I am not giving you a tip. I played the 'I don't have money / I am not sure what you are asking for' card. He went away, to sit around for a bit, and when he came back to lurk again, I just ignored him.

Tip, my arse.

We left the hotel at 3 am, an hour earlier than we needed to because we were wide awake. I expected the tuk-tuks to be lurking on the corner where drivers hassled us for business on a daily basis. There was one lonely tuk-tuk parked up for the night but no driver in sight.

Out of the gloom a man cycled his rickshaw towards us. He had a rough brown blanket wrapped around him for warmth. We had never seen the roads so quiet. It was still hazy and the rickshaw had no lights. We knew it wasn't far to the station and we quickly calculated that we had plenty of time to go by rickshaw, thereby giving the man some business and warming him up in the process. We piled up our suitcases and rucksacks on his rickshaw and squeezed onto the seat. He set off. When the road went slightly uphill we had to hop out and walk 50 m or so while he pushed the rickshaw, laden with luggage.

He had asked just 100 rupees for the fare. We paid him double which seemed to make his day. It still didn't seem enough. I wish now I had given him 1,000 rupees.

Crazy old Delhi

'If slaughterhouses had glass walls, everyone would
be a vegetarian'

—*Paul McCartney*

6 December 2018

*Trying to doze on the bed. Knackered. My mind playing
out images of Delhi today. I feel angry, sad, enraged,
furious, frustrated, helpless...*

*I can't believe it but I literally sit upright in bed, as if pro-
pelled by some inner force, tears in my eyes. No, wait a
minute. I am not totally helpless. I can speak up about the
slaughter and appalling treatment of millions of animals
every single day.*

*In the US alone, 300 animals die every second... 300,
600, 900. I will not contribute to those kind of statistics any
more.*

So what was it really that, on Thursday 6 December, so
bothered me?

❧

Most tourists, when they arrive on package tours in Delhi, are taken to Jama Masjid, one of the largest mosques in India which can accommodate 25,000 people in its court-yard, and from there they are ushered to a cycle rickshaw for an exciting ride through the bustling, colourful, potholed streets of Old Delhi. For anyone's first experience of India, it is exhilarating indeed.

We did that a few years ago (I even did it when I was 19), we took in Jama Masjid, Himayun's Tomb and Qutb Minar and voilà, you can tick the box and say you have 'done' Delhi.

We have always wanted to explore Old Delhi at our own pace and after three months of being in India we found it an easy thing to do. Our plan was not to have a plan, other than to walk like it wasn't our first time, to let ourselves get lost down alleys, occasionally asking the general direction of a main landmark and saying 'namaste' to all the street sellers and school children.

In addition to all that, we booked two different tours to learn a bit more about the city, one cycling, one walking, both of them brilliant, enlightening and eye-opening.

After the DelhiByCycle tour, we walked through some more crazy lanes before finding ourselves on Chandni Chowk and opted for the first international brand-name air-conditioned trustworthy (not gonna get sick at this late stage) restaurant for a cold drink. We felt a bit guilty going into such a place, but neither of us was in the mood to faff about looking for alternatives. There, as we looked out on to the street, I was ready to burst into tears, trying to process all we had seen in a few hours.

It took me by surprise. I was not sure why India had suddenly got to me after all this time. Old Delhi was all

I loved about the place and all I hated. It had been challenging on every level, physically, mentally and emotionally. And this day it had taken me too far. A lot had to do with animals.

First thing in the morning, we had cycled down a butchering street, where there were dozens of small slaughterhouses. We hadn't been warned about it. As it dawned on me, I tried not to look but I glimpsed one skip-load of goats' heads and one skip-load of freshly cut trotters. We were told that by 9 am all the butchering would be finished, the meat would be sent out for sale and the shopfronts would be closed. Later, when we went down the same road, the shutters were down and you would not know that you were in such a murderous place, unless you could guess why the puddles were red.

A little further along, a child as young as six, sitting at the side of the road, was slitting livers. I thought he was doing it carelessly until I realised that he was holding a sharp knife between his toes and then tossing the meat into a bowl.

Further on, there was a man holding a small length of rope attached to a plump goat. I could only assume that it was the goat's last day in this world and he was destined for the market. Another goat, on a chain at the side of the road, was somewhat startled by all the noise but was briefly calmed by our words and a brief pat on her nose and ears. I prayed she was being kept for milk.

Onwards through the lanes, and we had seen enough chickens in cages already. I saw men picking up live chickens by the feet and transferring them from a van to a cage in a shop. There is no dignified way to pick up a chicken at times like this and luckily the man showed no extra brutality. It was distressing enough as it was.

Suddenly to my left, I caught sight of a vendor holding up a chicken and he had his hands around its neck. I looked away just in time and I quickly covered my ears so I didn't hear anything that would stop me sleeping at night. I actually blurted something out loud. 'Oh no, not in front of me. God. This place.'

We cycled to the banks of the Yamuna River. Trying to ignore the rubbish, we enjoyed the spectacle of thousands of migratory birds. They swirled around in a huge swathe of movement and got particularly raucous when a small boat pushed out from the riverbank. It's considered good luck to feed the birds after cremations which happened further upstream.

From there, we took a short walk to a cow sanctuary. A sanctuary. It's supposed to be a good place, but the cows and calves were covered in mud, the calves had tiny lengths of rope and there were so many cows in one stable they could hardly move. I had so many questions and so little time. I didn't see a staff member to ask more about what went on here.

Jains, now they seem to be a nice religion, very loving of all living things, though there are some who take it too far. There are some Jains in Delhi who choose not to wear clothes for fear of having harmed a creature. We wanted to visit the Digambara Jain temple but it had closed for the afternoon. Behind it was a charitably run bird hospital where we saw this sign: 'Birds are our friends: Do not hunt them for your food, amusement and pleasure. Safety and security of our living creatures and environment is our topmost religion.'

If only everyone in India could be Jain, what a different world we might live in. They had separated the 'veg' and 'non-veg' birds. There was a disabled white rabbit with its neck to one side, but it seemed happy enough, especially when it was touched. There was no one to show us around so we consulted Lonely Planet, which said that the hospital was established 'to further the Jain principle of preserving all life, with a capacity of 10,000. Only vegetarian birds are admitted (up to 60 per day), though predators are treated as outpatients'.

We ended up at the 'world-famous' Karim's for breakfast. Hands up who is now vegetarian, someone joked as they asked who had spotted what was going on in the butchering street. Luckily there was a vegetarian option, even though this was a restaurant that was proud of its traditional meat specialities. They were happy to boast these old reviews (I include their errors):

From the Los Angeles Times in 1985:
'Over the years Karim's has become famous for its flat, hot tandoori breads, mutton curries, barbecue chicken and other specially dishes that include sheep-brain curry and foot-of-goat soup, paaye, which is served only for breakfast and is said to have restorative powers similar to those of Mexican menudo.'

(Paaye or paya are trotters, which could be from a cow, goat, buffalo or sheep. Menudo is a traditional Mexican dish made from the stomach of a cow. Yum yum.)

From BBC World Guide in 1994:
'... recommend meat-eaters to try Karim's... for a traditional breakfast of spice goats' totters... better than the bacons & eggs and more delicious.'

※

What else had got to me, I wondered. Well, if it wasn't animals, it was humans. What on earth is India going to do about its over-population? The worst deformities, beggars, men traipsing past with their uncombed hair matted with dust, with literally just the shirt on their back, trousers which have no crotch any more, clothes which are no more than rags, and shoes which someone else would have thrown away 30 years ago. It was somehow sadder than being barefoot.

Early in the morning we saw hundreds of men sitting on the kerbside waiting for a free meal from the Gurudwara Bangla Sahib. The Sikhs serve 10,000 at the temple every day. Later, when the food was ready, the crowd surged forward and there was no space between each man as they were given what was perhaps their only meal of the day.

Which is all why, when it comes to the pantomime that is bartering for your tuk-tuk ride, even I had mellowed. As our journey progressed, we rarely took even 50 rupees off the price, because we realised that what we were paying for a fare was peanuts. We knew that what we were being asked for was probably ten times the locals' rate just because of the colour of our skin but, in reality, a couple of quid for a relatively long journey, certainly one we didn't want to do on foot in the heat and pollution, was actually very cheap.

We learned that the average tuk-tuk driver makes 400 rupees per day. That's about £4. Even in India, that really doesn't go far. Also, most tuk-tuks are rented, so drivers will most likely have to pay their 'boss' a fee.

The walking tour we did with Street Connections. It was really the best way to get to places you wouldn't normally see and to hear more about life in the city. We chose the tour because it gives something back to the community. Our guide Lalit was once a street child himself. His mother died when he was two months old, his father died when he was five. Although he and his older sister were taken in by a neighbour, they weren't treated well so he ran away. He ended up in Delhi. He teamed up with another kid and started rag picking but he also got into drugs and petty theft. (He was still a very young child at the time.) When caught by the police he was given two options — go back to your home town or go to the Salaam Baalak shelter. He did the latter. Although he found it tough, he was delighted to be getting three decent meals a day. He was also going to be educated.

Every day around 140 children arrive in one of the four railway stations in the capital. What are they running from that is so bad? And what risks do they face in the underbelly of Delhi, where there is crime, exploitation and sexual abuse? The Salaam Baalak Trust (www.salaambaalaktrust. com), established in 1988 with the proceeds of the film Salaam Bombay, operates 18 centres in Delhi alone. It aims to give street children the five basics every child should have: food, security, health, education and love.

Lalit took us through the lanes of Old Delhi, past weird and wonderful sights, havelis and temples, trees growing across alleyways, monkeys crossing the wires above us. We were shown a factory where a dozen men were busy at sewing machines. The boss was around and although on the surface he seemed pleasant enough I got the feeling that no one wanted to look up from their work for fear of the consequences. They worked a 12-hour day with just a half-hour lunch break, for which they were paid 300 rupees a day, roughly £3. In most cases the men are away from home and their families are hundreds of kilometres away in rural villages. I wondered how they could afford to send money home. They even share rented rooms so as to cut costs to the very minimum and be able to buy some food. At least, I suppose, they have a job.

Elsewhere, work in Old Delhi is impossibly physical, men pulling and pushing overloaded barrows, cycle rickshaws, great packages on their heads. I noticed that with most of these labourers, their eyes had glazed over. We wondered what mental and physical health issues they had — but probably had to ignore.

At home, our autistic friends often speak of sensory overload, moments when everybody in the world seems to be talking at once. Delhi in rush-hour, which was most of the time, was enough to give anyone sensory overload, what with its cacophony of traffic, heat and poor air quality. It certainly illustrated the enormous issue of overcrowding. Where do all these people go at night? How do they get through each day?

India gives you a spiritual journey, whether you like it or not. There is something about the country which makes you question your place in this life and how you are living it. People who know and love India will understand this. In Delhi, I realised that part of what I love about India is that it moves me, usually when I am least expecting it. It might be a group of men walking through the streets holding aloft a stretcher carrying a dead body covered in marigold garlands. It can be the exquisite beauty of a carving in an ancient temple. It can be a scruffy dog dozing in the middle of a pile of rubbish. It can be a young beggar child giving you a wide smile. Or it can be the exhilarating tuk-tuk ride through a narrow, dirty, dusty, potholed street, narrowly missing people, dogs, cows and street sellers.

India certainly makes you feel alive.

We walked to Kinari Market. Most tourists who arrive by coach for a tour of Old Delhi will take a cycle rickshaw from outside Jama Masjid to be taken along the street where the shops are packed with colourful fabrics, jewellery and garlands. When we were one of those tourists in 2014, I didn't know it was called Kinari Market. We had loved our brief taste of India so much that we decided that our children should see it. Two years later, we started our adventure in Delhi, staying at a modest hotel in a residential district called Karol Bagh. As we had driven in, David had noticed that the busy main street was lined with an eclectic mix of waifs and strays.

At dinner that first night he suggested getting up early the next morning to do some street photography. He pitched it in a way that the children would be doing him a favour because he didn't want to go alone laden with an expensive camera or two. In reality, he wanted them to witness real life on the streets of downtown Delhi.

They were met by the sight of what seemed like a mile of people under makeshift tarpaulins, sheets and blankets. A colourful mix of the very old, the very young, human and canine. Small piles of rubbish had been lit to provide warmth in the surprisingly cool morning air and to warm the cups of chai. Many people were still asleep on dirty scraps of cardboard, within sight of hotels, banks and jewellery wholesalers. Two teenage boys slept with their arms around each other and David said his stomach churned as he noticed the flies settling on their lips and around their eyes.

When we visited the slums of Mumbai on this trip, we had clumsily referred to the poor people living in such conditions. Our guide told us that the slum dwellers were not poor people. They had a roof over their heads, walls to keep out most of the dangers and access to a toilet albeit 200 m away and shared with 20 other families. These people living in the slums had jobs, family units, a sense of community. The 'poor' people were the ones living on the streets, under park benches, in urine-sodden doorways, on top of bus shelters, where the children fall prey to a myriad dangers, traffic fumes, predatory adults seeking sex, child traffickers, cold, hunger and disease. On the street they mingle with mangy dogs and wandering cattle. It's grim.

I am not sure where the inspiration came from to share everything we love about India with our children, but it turned out to be one of our finest decisions. In 2016, the seven of us had an adventure in a minibus on a packed itinerary, a week in India and a week in Nepal.

My daughter was covered in henna against her will at India Gate, one of our group asked a guide who Gandhi was, another walked like a constipated duck when he had Delhi Belly (he was anything but constipated), there was terror from the girls when a crocodile snapped its jaws close to us in Chitwan National Park (the dugout canoe suddenly felt very flimsy), and there was the time when someone sneezed in the back of the minibus en route to Pokhara and a bogey landed splat on the open book being held by his step-brother. You couldn't make it up.

Memories were made from mealtime conversations as much as sightseeing. Highlights included games of politically incorrect Cards Against Humanity with a few beers on a rooftop in Kathmandu while thunder rumbled around overhead.

The best moment, however, was being able to stand in front of the Taj Mahal at sunrise with all of our adult children. A special and privileged memory indeed.

The greatest peaceful
revolution ever known

'Until we extend our circle of compassion to all living
things, humanity will not find peace'

—*Albert Schweitzer*

We sat on a bench to rest. We had been walking for an hour,
up and down on the winding cliff path. We were wrapped up
against the brisk wind. We had warmed up nicely but we
knew to keep the layers on while we paused to enjoy the
view. We peered down sheer slopes of heather and gorse to
the granite rocks below. We observed how unspoilt the path
was, how fresh the air and how quiet the afternoon had been.
We had passed just one runner and a couple with a dog. The
winter sun, just strong enough to make itself felt on your
face, was shimmering on a dark blue sea.

We looked across the water and could see France on the
horizon. Our dog was at our feet. We were home.

There is a question which every traveller gets asked over and over. Not 'Where are you going?' but 'Where are you from?'

Over the six months that we had been away, it was often easier to reply 'England' than 'Jersey'. 'Lovely jubbly,' the taxi and tuk-tuk drivers would respond. 'London. Manchester,' as if they were the only two places that we might come from.

Occasionally, however, we would proudly say: 'Jersey.' And then we would have to explain a bit more. Close to France. World Cup winners, yes. You've heard of New Jersey? We're old Jersey. No, not American. British. No, we are not part of the United Kingdom and we are not part of the European Union. Yes, a bit of a constitutional oddity, you could say. A Crown Dependency.

I have always known that Jersey is special and before we left on our 32,000 km journey, we doubted that we would find anywhere better than our home island. Truth be told, we didn't, but that is not to say we didn't enjoy our travels. Far from it. We appreciated everything it had thrown at us.

In return, we got that re-boot, a rethink of life, a feel for being young and energised, a desire for 'back to basics' when we got home, the realisation that, apart from travel, what matters in our life is family and being at home with a dog and a cat. And, something else I knew already, we are privileged indeed to live in Jersey.

The kids were missing us, we were missing Zippy, and it was time to go home, for the start of a new journey, one of compassion, and love for animals and care for our planet. Ahimsa, here we come.

Zippy quickly forgave us for being away all that time. Initially he was a bit aloof but we reckoned it was because we had a different smell, not least thanks to the long journey home. We like to think that he knew that we had been on a special journey. God knows we have told him enough about all the sick and injured dogs we met.

We arrived home refreshed. Any niggly aches and pains and minor menopausal symptoms had disappeared. They just didn't seem to be worth worrying about when measured against the world's problems. And, quite bizarrely, my index fingers had stopped twisting into arthritic witchy digits. In fact, the process seemed to have reversed. Imperceptible at the time but wonderful to notice on a cold winter's day.

We arrived home with two weeks to go until Christmas Day. Two weeks to plan and prepare a plant-based feast for the family. No turkey. No pigs in blankets. No goose fat. With no job to go to until the new year, I had time to clear the kitchen cupboards in time for Veganuary. A new journey was indeed starting.

The word 'vegetarianism' was coined in the 1840s. Before that, vegetarians were referred to as Pythagoreans after the Greek philosopher Pythagoras, who lived from 570-490 BC. He said: 'As long as man continues to be the ruthless destroyer of lower living beings, he will never know health or peace. For as long as men massacre animals, they will kill each other. Indeed, he who sows the seeds of murder and pain cannot reap joy and love.'

Victor Hugo, who was once exiled in Jersey, shortly before writing Les Misérables, once said something which has been roughly translated as: 'There is nothing more powerful than an idea whose time has come.'

In 2019, the time came for veganism.

When we decided to go vegan, we didn't realise just how topical veganism would be. I signed up to Veganuary, which inspires people around the world to try a vegan diet for a month. Although it takes place all year round, most people give it a go in January. Run by a UK-registered charity, it is dedicated to changing public attitudes and behaviours, while providing all the information and practical support required to make the transition as easy and enjoyable as possible.

In 2019, according to the Veganuary organisers, more than 250,000 people took part, more than ever before. This compares to 168,500 in 2018 and just 59,500 in 2017. The top three countries getting involved were the UK, the USA and India. I was delighted to read that Mumbai and Delhi made the top 20 cities. According to www.veganuary. com, 28% of the people who pledged to take part in 2019 were aged 25-34 and for the first time it was health that was given as the main reason, ahead of animals and climate change.

I found their Facebook page to be a wonderful place of positivity, support, suggestions, recommendations, recipes and debating points. Being connected to vegans old and new around the world was part of the joy of the first month.

I started cooking more and, instead of seeing it as a chore, I actually enjoyed it. I realise now that I never did like the smell of raw pork or the feel of raw chicken or handling a turkey carcass. I expected people to be more challenging of my decision but that did not happen. They asked questions but no one said they didn't think I should be doing it. I was really quite disappointed that I wasn't asked where I get my protein and B12 from, because I was ready with the answers. (Would you ever ask a pregnant gorilla whether she gets enough protein?)

It is estimated that the number of animals spared thanks to people doing Veganuary in 2019 was nearly 60 million. Quite apart from animals saved, Veganuary, in 2019 particularly, got people talking — even Piers Morgan when he made a fuss about Greggs' vegan sausage rolls, and that can only be a good thing.

David and I had a huge advantage in that our tastebuds had changed subtly without our noticing, so when we got home we went straight to dairy-free versions of milk, cheese and chocolate. I was surprised that I enjoyed them all, but I appreciate that people who try to make the change overnight from their favourite brand to a vegan version might not like them. It seems that vegan cheese, particularly, doesn't quite cut it for a lot of people. I also didn't think I would successfully move across to soya lattes and mint tea. But I did. Going vegan has not been a hardship, but a pleasure.

If you think it is just lentils and nuts, you are sorely mistaken. In my first month alone I made lasagne, pastry-topped mushroom and courgette pie, a wonderful stir-fry of leftover vegetables and pak choi, a 'shepherdless' pie, a satay sweet potato curry, aloo gobi, pizza, fruit cake, lemon drizzle and a coconut cheesecake. My plate came alive with colour and flavour, not a dull slab of dead animal.

Having learned that about one third of all food produced globally goes to waste, I also made greater efforts not to throw away so much and I found it increasingly easy to whip up soups and stir-fries out of leftovers. We discovered nooch, aquafaba and seitan. Even David started adding seeds to his porridge, which is not something I ever thought I would say.

Many people are likely to be concerned that it is more expensive to be vegan. Certainly, some products are pricey, nuts particularly, but most of your normal recipes can be 'veganised' at no great expense. It can balance out with the savings made on the basics of veg, lentils and rice.

We entered a world of reading labels, which is interesting, challenging and at first doesn't half slow down your weekly shop. But before you know it, it becomes second nature. Some products are obviously not vegan, but there is much which is not so clearcut. Isinglass, pepsin, gelatine, albumen — all to be avoided and easily remembered. But there are E-number nasties, like E542: ground-up animal bones used to keep food moist. Or how about E910, 920, 921, an additive called L-cysteine made from animal hair and feathers, found in some breads as an improving agent. Once you know what's in your mass-produced food, it's not so difficult really.

You don't have to like everything, of course. I admit that 'pulses and grains' don't sound particularly appetising and I don't care for quinoa. I'm not a fan of fake meat and particularly dislike the idea of bleeding burgers, but if it works for you and saves another animal, go for it. More than anything, adopting a vegan diet is a mindset. I asked David if he missed bacon and eggs. No, he replied, we don't need it in our lives. If you tell yourself you can't live without bacon, then you'll find it tough. If you tell yourself that you don't need it and don't want it (and you know how the pig is likely to have been treated in life and in death), it becomes a whole lot easier. Besides, I have always thought that the smell of bacon promised more than it delivered. Same with a barbecue.

I know that I will make mistakes and I know that animals will have been used and abused for many more products including medication, cosmetics, toiletries and cleaning products. I am still educating myself on those matters.

It takes time. And I know there will be other burning questions, like: Will I drink non-vegan wine? What do I feed my dog? Do I wear wool? (If you are interested in reading up on that one online, read PETA's answer to the question 'What's wrong with wool?')

For me, veganism was not just a fad, a new year resolution which was going to peter out by mid-February. It was a whole lifestyle change, and it's for life.

Mine and theirs.

'In all the round world of Utopia there is no meat. There used to be. But now we cannot stand the thought of slaughter-houses… And it is practically impossible to find anyone who will hew a dead ox or pig… I can still remember, as a boy, the rejoicings over the closing of the last slaughter-house.'

HG Wells wrote that in 1905, in A Modern Utopia.

What happens in animal farming around the world every single day is horrifying. Sows are confined to crates barely bigger than their own bodies until they give birth. They cannot even turn around. They can't nuzzle their new piglets. When the young are taken from the mother, she will be impregnated again and the whole miserable cycle continues.

Chickens are selectively bred to grow unnaturally fast, which means their legs can't support their bodies. Up to 19 broilers can be packed into just one square metre, less than an A4 page per bird. They get skin diseases and burns from ammonia because they live in their own filth.

Ethically sourced, organic 'happy meat' isn't any better. In fact, it can actually be less environmentally sound because a lot more land is needed to raise them and grass-fed animals emit significantly more methane, which causes global warming. And the bottom line is, those animals did not live out their natural lives and they certainly did not want to die just so that you could enjoy a beef casserole or roast pork.

A documentary about farming practice made me realise just how much suffering there is in the dairy and egg industries. We like to think of our beautiful Jersey cows grazing in the countryside and I am pretty confident that in our island we have as near best practice as possible. But we mustn't kid ourselves about the facts.

In any dairy industry, a cow is artificially inseminated to make her have a calf more times than she would naturally in her lifetime. If that calf is male, it will be slaughtered. It doesn't matter to my argument how it is slaughtered, though I doubt it will be put down gently the way a loved pet would be. It is a life which is considered worthless. Sometimes it gets to live a little longer before being slaughtered and sold as 'baby beef'.

And even with so-called best practice, these are the facts that milk-drinkers choose to ignore. According to the Government of Jersey's Rural Economy Strategy 2017-2021:

'The knacker's service operates five days per week, providing a slaughter and disposal service for livestock. Livestock are usually slaughtered on the farm of origin and carcasses are transported to the knacker's yard for incineration. Operation on a Saturday is intended to ensure that male calves born over the weekend are dispatched within 36 hours of birth. During 2016, the knacker's service disposed of an average of 40 calves, five cows, three sheep, one pig and one horse per week.

'The incinerator in 2016 was also used to dispose of 142 tonnes of abattoir waste, 16 tonnes of spent hens and any livestock killed by the knacker's service, as well as any carcasses found washed up on Jersey's shore (eg dolphins, seals, etc).'

Let that sink in a moment. Jersey's world-famous dairy industry: On average, 40 calves slaughtered every single week. That's more than 2,000 per year.

Scale it up for most bigger dairy industries in the UK.

The mother's natural instinct to protect and love each one of those calves matters not one bit to the farmer nor, it seems, to the consumer. We know the mother suffers mentally. And then humans take her milk, the milk that was supposed to feed her baby. Even if the calf is female and kept for future milking, the mother and calf will be separated unnaturally and distressingly early, often within 24 hours, so that humans can have the milk.

It's cruel, particularly when there are now so many excellent alternatives (soya, oat, almond, hazelnut, cashew, rice, coconut) and they're readily available. It's only when you stop to think about it that the whole idea of drinking another species' lactations is pretty weird. And just because we have always done it doesn't mean that we always should. There was a time when slavery was ok, when women didn't have the vote, when people smoked cigarettes in workplaces, when homosexuality was illegal. All of it unthinkable now.

For quite a time on the home straight towards veganism, we convinced ourselves that we could still eat eggs. Surely hens are happy and, if you choose the free-range ones, spend their time in lovely sunny fields? And then we read about what happens to male chicks which, being of no use to the egg farm, get macerated live in a grinder. Live! Killing male chicks happens regardless of whether the egg is produced in a free-range system or from a caged battery hen.

There will always be people who want to take issue with the vegan viewpoint. They may argue that maceration does not happen in the UK, where the chicks are more likely to be gassed. Does that really make it any better?

Vegans get angry, sad and frustrated, simply because they have learned what is going on. Because animals can't speak for themselves. Because, actually, we don't need to eat animals any more.

Everyone says that they care about the planet these days. But do they? Everyone shares a Facebook post by Sir David Attenborough about climate change or the state of our oceans and yet they carry on eating fish. Can they not make the connection? People make a fuss about plastic bags or straws because of the danger they pose to sea-life, and yet most of those people still eat fish. Humans catching fish is a greater danger to sea-life than a straw ever was.

Abandoned fishing gear is the biggest killer in the ocean, claiming the lives of whales, dolphins, turtles, sharks, crabs and, of course, fish. The oceans are getting increasingly toxic and chemicals ingested by fish are getting into our food chain. Lex Rigby, writing for Viva!, says: 'Shellfish lovers are eating up to 11,000 plastic fragments in their seafood each year and a third of UK-caught fish, including cod, haddock, mackerel and shellfish, were found to be contaminated with plastic.'

Some scientists claim that, at current rates of decline, the oceans could be devoid of fish by 2048. That is astonishing. No fish — within my lifetime? As I see it, every meal is part of the problem, however the fish was caught.

More than 150 million land animals are killed for food around the world every day.

David and I have always enjoyed eating out and we are certainly spoilt for choice for restaurants in Jersey. Admittedly, eating out as a vegan is more awkward than before, mainly because there is less choice, but it's improving all the time.

I have no doubt that veganism will be normalised, just like vegetarian and gluten-free already are. I look forward to the day when it's the meat eaters who are the ones who are considered odd and have to make special requests. I dream of a time when school dinners, hospital food and corporate catering are all by default plant-based, all of it perfectly nutritious and delicious. All it requires is a shift in thinking.

In fact, it seems to be heading that way, slowly. In 2018 the Vegan Society petitioned the UK Government to ensure that plant-based options are available on public sector menus every day. After all, once all the current batch of vegans grows older, we will need it as standard in hospitals and old people's homes.

As a vegan, you are very aware of the marketing of food products on a daily basis, in advertising, in shops, on TV. In my local supermarket I see a poster which declares 'A better life for animals'. I see meat labelled 'RSPCA approved'. Jersey Dairy says: 'We know that happy cows produce more milk so ours have their own latex mattresses to sleep on and back scratchers to keep them relaxed!'

All this is merely marketing designed to make you feel better about eating meat or drinking milk, but it doesn't really make it better for animals at all.

Ultimately, moves towards veganism will have to be commercially led. We don't want to see people lose their livelihoods but we would like to see farmers adapt without having to slaughter the innocent. Farmers can diversify. The animals don't have a choice. They don't have a voice. They are the ones who are suffering.

I look forward to seeing the first dairy farmer in Jersey having the guts to stop production and let their herd be available for cow cuddling. Recent studies have shown that cuddling up to a cow is beneficial to our mental health. Certainly, I can vouch for the fact that cows are very beautiful, gentle creatures who are wonderful to hug. Medication for the soul indeed.

Veganism, of course, is not just a food choice, it is a lifestyle. The Vegan Society defines it as 'a way of living which seeks to exclude, as far as is possible and practicable, all forms of exploitation of, and cruelty to, animals for food, clothing or any other purpose'.

I used to buy bags and shoes based on price and design. Now, there is a third (and most important) factor — what they are made from. It just seems a natural progression and it is easy enough to find the alternatives, both in shops locally and online. I am switching brands of cosmetics and toiletries as and when they need replacing. After all, every single purchase is a vote to put an end to animal cruelty.

'The most violent weapon on earth is the table fork'
— Mahatma Gandhi

⚜

In our time away, we became big fans of Gandhi and all that
he stood for, and this was reinforced when we read what he
had to say about eating animals. As a Vaishnava, one of the
major Hindu denominations, he was a vegetarian. Indeed, in
1888, aged 18, when he left India to go to the UK, he vowed
not to touch wine, women and meat. It was only when he did
this that he got his mother's permission to travel. Being vegetarian in England at that time was difficult and he was often
ridiculed but, living on a limited budget, he found it to be
cheap. When he learned about the misery suffered by cows
and buffaloes, he gave up milk too.

It would only take a few more influential leaders to bring
about significant change. In 2019, Pope Francis was challenged to go vegan for Lent. In exchange, he was offered
$1 million to give to a charity of his choice. The call came
from animal rights activist Genesis Butler, then 12, and the
Million Dollar Vegan campaign. In an open letter, she wrote:
'Your Holiness, we must act. Moving towards a plant-based
diet will have substantial environmental benefits. It will
protect our land, trees, oceans, and air, and help feed the
world's most vulnerable.'

Sadly, it doesn't look like he did it, but it brings us on to
all the other great reasons for going vegan. According to the
United Nations Food and Agriculture Organisation, farmed
animals contribute 14.5% of human-generated greenhouse
gas emissions, which is more than every car, plane, truck
and train on the planet.

In 2018, in their paper 'Reducing food's environmental impacts through producers and consumers', Oxford University researchers Joseph Poore and Thomas Nemecek said that going vegan was the single biggest way we can reduce our environmental impact on the planet. Eating a plant-based diet cuts greenhouse gas emissions, reduces pollution and water usage, prevents deforestation and saves wild animals from extinction.

Referring to the study, which was published in the journal Science, as 'the most comprehensive analysis to date of the damage farming does to the planet', the Guardian reported: 'The new research shows that without meat and dairy consumption, global farmland use could be reduced by more than 75% – an area equivalent to the US, China, European Union and Australia combined – and still feed the world. Loss of wild areas to agriculture is the leading cause of the current mass extinction of wildlife.'

Veganuary reports that the meat industry is also the leading cause of ocean dead zones – areas of sea which have zero oxygen. What a dreadful thought.

Deforestation, dead zones, species going extinct... and it could all be stopped or reduced by our own actions, our own choices. As Earthling Ed says: 'Time and time again, science is showing us that we have the power in our own hands to change the world.'

A plant-based diet is also healthier, of course, which makes it a particularly good thing to be thinking about as we get older. In 2017 the British Dietetic Association (www. bda.uk.com) confirmed that a well-planned vegan diet can support healthy living in people of all ages, including during pregnancy and breastfeeding.

Within three months of being vegan, my cholesterol was already lower and, now that you and I are on toilet terms,

I can vouch for the fact that you are unlikely ever to be constipated again.

Only when the last tree has died
and the last river has been poisoned
and the last fish been caught
will we realise we cannot eat money

– Indian proverb

I haven't even mentioned other hideous animal cruelty the world over, bull-fighting, greyhound racing, seal slaughter, fur and skins for fashion, animals used for cosmetic-testing, beagles force-fed pesticides, the list always seems so terrifyingly endless. Now that I have signed a few petitions in campaigns against animal cruelty, I hear about atrocities on a daily basis. Social media doesn't let us ignore it. Nor should it. We shouldn't scroll past without a thought, however much it pains us. We should use social media as a force for good and for achieving change fast.

One person can make a difference, just like the man who threw the starfish back into the sea. It's estimated that by going vegan, you can save 100 lives per year. If I reach 85, which I sincerely hope I do, I could save 3,000 lives. If all seven members of my close family were also vegan, together we could save 24,000 animals. That makes it worth doing, doesn't it? I am proud that my first grandchild is being brought up as a herbivore. Having taken action in our own household, at least now we can sleep at night knowing we are doing what we can — and I will be able to tell Aurora what I did when she asks me about the animal holocaust.

Donald Watson once described a life-changing moment of his childhood. 'Then the day came when one of the pigs was killed: I still have vivid recollections of the whole process – including the screams, of course. One thing that shocked me was that my Uncle George, of whom I thought very highly, was part of the crew. I decided that farms – and uncles – had to be reassessed: the idyllic scene was nothing more than Death Row, where every creature's days were numbered by the point at which it was no longer of service to human beings.'

It's now more than 75 years since Mr Watson formed the Vegan Society. He said: 'The vegan believes that if we are to be true emancipators of animals we must renounce absolutely our traditional and conceited attitude that we have the right to use them to serve our needs. We must supply these needs by other means... If the vegan ideal of non-exploitation was generally adopted, it would be the greatest peaceful revolution ever known, abolishing vast industries and establishing new ones in the better interests of men and animals alike.'

I am proud to be part of a great peaceful revolution. It's odd that vegans get accused of propaganda, when we are the ones who simply want an end to suffering and slaughter. The vitriol levelled at vegans can be quite astounding.

It's time that everyone started thinking about the impact we are having on Earth and other species. Not making the change because they have to. Not because they feel coerced into it. But because they want to. They want to make a difference. They want to be healthier and be part of this exciting peaceful revolution.

This is not an academic book. This is a book by a mother and grandmother who likes travelling and writing. People can put forward as many arguments and obstacles as they like when challenged to consider veganism but ultimately, for me, it boils down simply to one question.

When you have access to meat-, dairy- and egg-free alternatives, why would you not choose them over the ones that cause harm, suffering and death?

Ahimsa is the highest virtue, Ahimsa is the highest self-control,
Ahimsa is the greatest gift, Ahimsa is the best suffering,
Ahimsa is the highest sacrifice, Ahimsa is the finest strength,
Ahimsa is the greatest friend, Ahimsa is the greatest happiness,
Ahimsa is the highest truth, and Ahimsa is the greatest teaching.
— The Mahabharata, Sanskrit epic of Ancient India

Tips for New Vegans

1. Be easy on yourself. If you make a mistake, so be it. It doesn't mean you should give up.
2. Don't rush out buying flax seeds, freekeh and brown lentils. Start with dishes you know and love and 'vegan-ise' them. Have fun shopping around and discovering different products in different supermarkets, health stores and Asian markets.
3. It is only as difficult as you want to make it. Make a list of all the things you *can* eat and start from there.
4. Have a few staple dinner party meals. I like to keep them simple but effective, something tasty and filling which will satisfy any meat eater.
5. Not everyone goes vegan overnight. It may take weeks or months of transition, and that's ok too.
6. Surround yourself with positive people, such as local vegan Facebook groups, where you can get tips, recipes, restaurant recommendations and encouragement when/ if you find it difficult.
7. If you're not sure where to begin, try giving up meat for Lent, or try committing to one month for Veganuary. If nothing else, it opens the discussion with others. The more people who stop and think about what they eat, the better.

8. If you think friends or family might not be supportive, you don't even have to use the V word. Go for 'plant-based' and just say you're doing it for your health. They are less likely to argue with that.

9. Start replacing cosmetics, toiletries and cleaning materials, making the switch to environmentally friendly products not tested on animals. I have done this on an item by item basis, deciding that just throwing away what I already have would be wasteful. In a similar vein, I think it's ok to keep a much-loved pair of leather shoes or favourite handbag, but commit to never buying real leather or suede again.

10. Thinking of giving in to temptation? Remind yourself why you want to be vegan and watch one of the powerful documentaries like Dominion or Earthlings to keep you on track.

Book Club Questions

1. Has reading the book changed your mind about anything, such as eating meat, riding elephants or interacting with beggars?

2. The author describes her relationship with Zippy. Has an animal ever changed your life? Do you understand the love of a dog or cat?

3. Is it the kind of journey you would like to undertake? Could you go away for six months with your partner/spouse or would they drive you crazy?

4. The author writes: 'What's the difference between tortoise on the menu in Vietnam and crab or lobster on the menu at home? What is the difference between a spit-roast dog in Hanoi and a hog roast at a summer party?' Discuss.

5. When should you walk past and when should you say something? Have you ever been on holiday and got angry about something you have seen, such as the welfare of horses or donkeys? Did you speak up?

6. What examples of support and/or obstacles would you expect from your nearest and dearest when introducing big changes to your lifestyle and philosophy? Do you pursue those changes regardless or should you compromise?

7. What should we be thinking about when we travel? Should we be considering our own tourism footprint? How do you think tourism might change in the future?

8. Which passages or characters were particularly memorable?

Notes

The first names of some of the people we met have been changed.

Chapter 1
The video which brought us to Udaipur: https://animal aidunlimited.org/blog/wounded-dog-staggering-in-traffic-saved/

Chapter 2
Our blog: kidswontleavehome.blog

Chapter 3
Soi Dog Foundation (www.soidog.org)
Sapiens: A Brief History of Mankind by Yuval Noah Harari, published by Harper

Chapter 4
Elephant Nature Park (www.elephantnaturepark.org)

Chapter 5
Animals Asia (www.animalsasia.org)

Chapter 6
Most of Vietnam's 25 species of tortoise and turtle are threatened: https://vietnam.wcs.org/Wildlife/turtle-and-tortoise.aspx

Chapter 9
Deaths and injuries caused by live munitions and landmines:
http://www.mekong.net/cambodia/mines.htm

40,000 people live as amputees: http://www.seasite.niu.edu/
khmer/Ledgerwood/Landmines.htm

First They Killed My Father by Luong Ung published by
Harper Perennial

Chapter 13
'Be the change that you wish to see in the world': It's
another quote from the late great Mahatma Gandhi

Chapter 16
Excerpt from AAU manual reproduced with the kind
permission of Erika Adams
Animal Aid Unlimited (www.animalaidunlimited.org)
Our Airbnb in Udaipur: Chandra Niwas (www.chandraniwas.
com)
Night-time bioluminescence walks: https://www.jersey
walkadventures.co.uk/wp-content/uploads/2010/05/Night-
time-guided-bioluminescence-walks-in-Jersey-pdf434.jpg

Chapter 19
AASRAA Trust (www.aasraatrust.org)
Gandhi: 'If we do not keep our back yards clean, our swaraj
will have a foul stench': https://pibindia.wordpress.com/
2017/01/13/swachh-bharat-mission-the-road-ahead/

Chapter 20
The Best Exotic Marigold Hotel by Deborah Moggach published by Penguin Random House

Chapter 21
There are nearly 800 mega-farms in the UK: https://www.theguardian.com/environment/2017/jul/17/uk-has-nearly-800-livestock-mega-farms-investigation-reveals

Humane Slaughter Association (www.hsa.org.uk):
'Every year in the UK approximately 2.6 million cattle, 10 million pigs, 14.5 million sheep and lambs, 80 million fish and 950 million birds are slaughtered for human consumption'

Chapter 22
Delirious Delhi by Dave Prager published by Arcade Publishing

Chapter 24
Pythagoreans: International Vegetarian Union: https://ivu.org/history/greece_rome/pythagoras.html

One third of all food produced globally goes to waste: http://www.fao.org/food-loss-and-food-waste/en/

What's wrong with wool? https://www.peta.org/living/personal-care-fashion/whats-wrong-wool/

Statistics from the knacker's service: States of Jersey's Rural Economy Strategy 2017-2021, published by the Department of Economic Development, Tourism, Sport and Culture and Department of the Environment

Lex Rigby is Campaigns Manager for Viva! (www.viva.org.uk), a charity working to end animal suffering

The oceans could be devoid of fish by 2048: https://www.nationalgeographic.com/animals/2006/11/seafood-biodiversity/

More than 150 million animals are killed for food around the world every day: https://brazil.sentientmedia.org/how-many-animals-are-killed-for-food-every-day/

In 2018 the Vegan Society petitioned the UK Government to ensure that plant-based options are available on public sector menus: https://www.vegansociety.com/whats-new/blog/government-petition-response-disappoints-vegans

Jersey Dairy says: 'We know that happy cows produce more milk so ours have their own latex mattresses to sleep on and back scratchers to keep them relaxed!': https://jerseydairy.com/about/our-cows/amazing-cow-facts/

Recent studies have shown that cuddling up to a cow is beneficial to mental health: https://www.bodyandsoul.com.au/mind-body/wellbeing/people-are-paying-to-cuddle-cows-in-the-name-of-mental-health/news-story/c39ea9dcc16fb7814dbadb1895e20801

As a Vaishnava, Gandhi was a vegetarian: https://www.veganfirst.com/article/did-mahatma-gandhi-quit-dairy-start-leading-a-vegan-life

Farmed animals contribute 14.5% of human-generated greenhouse gas emissions, which is more than every car, plane, truck and train on the planet: http://www.fao.org/3/a-i3437e.pdf

Poore and Nemecek: Going vegan is the single biggest way we can reduce our environmental impact on the planet: https://www.theguardian.com/environment/2018/may/31/avoiding-meat-and-dairy-is-single-biggest-way-to-reduce-your-impact-on-earth

Donald Watson once described a life-changing moment of his childhood: http://gentleworld.org/remembering-donald-watson-vegan-pioneer/

Recommended Viewing

Love & Bananas (www.loveandbananas.com) is available on iTunes and DVD. It tells the story of elephant rescue in Thailand.
Blackfish (www.blackfishmovie.com) is available on DVD.
The documentaries Land of Hope and Glory, Dominion, Cowspiracy and Earthlings are freely available online.
For more recommended documentaries, see: https://grainsgreensberriesbeans.wordpress.com/documentaries/
The Food Matrix — 101 Reasons to go Vegan is also available on YouTube.
Earthling Ed — You Will Never Look At Your Life The Same Way Again (no graphic footage): https://www.youtube.com/watch?v=Z3u7hXpOm58

Click on to www.vegancalculator.com to see how many thousands of animals are being slaughtered worldwide right now.

Acknowledgements

If my former editor, Chris Bright, had not leant forward over his coffee and told me that I should write a book, Ahimsa would never have happened. Thank you, Chris, for your comments, encouragement and never-ending ability to improve a sentence.

Thanks to those friends who share my enthusiasm for writing and to the family and friends who got to see some earlier drafts.

To all my family who have helped shape this life in one way or another, and particularly to all the teachers, club and community leaders and mentors who have 'been there' for Seb and Annie over the years, thank you. You have made a real difference to who they are today and I am so proud of them.

Thank you, Mum, for always letting me take chances and do what I need to do, even if you don't quite understand my love of travel, and particularly India.

To my sister, Nicola, you were right all along. Damn.

Particular thanks have to go to Animal Aid Unlimited, the AASRAA Trust and the Elephant Nature Park for the wonderful work they are carrying out every day, and to everyone who is going vegan and raising issues of animal welfare. Earthling Ed, I salute you.

And finally, thanks to David who shared the adventure. He has helped me see the world a different way, not least through our long, funny, frustrating and furious conversations over fried rice and Kingfisher beer about all the issues raised in the book. (I still haven't seen all of his 25,000 photographs.)

Oh, and Zippy. We love you.

About the Author

Caroline Earle is a former reporter, sub-editor and assistant editor of the Jersey Evening Post. The formative years of her 30-year career in local media were with BBC and commercial radio stations. She is currently a freelance writer for a magazine and works part-time for a charity which supports people with a disability or long-term health condition into employment. Caroline has previously worked as a fundraiser for an autism charity. She has two grown-up children, two stepsons, a daughter-in-law and one grandchild. They all live in Jersey in the Channel Islands. She lists travel, family and her rescue dog Zippy as her favourite things.